SETTING CAPTIVES FREE:
Purity Boot Camp Leader's Guide

— PURITY BOOT CAMP LEADER'S GUIDE —

MIKE CLEVELAND

SETTING CAPTIVE FREE
PUBLISHING

Cover Design: Melissa K. Thomas

Setting Captives Free Publishing
1400 W. Washington St., Ste. 104
Sequim, WA 98382

ISBN: 978-1-7337609-3-5
LCCN: 2019905223

Table of Contents

Encouragement

*B*efore you begin, we want to share the following testimony of a student who completed the Setting Captives Free Boot Camp course to encourage you in the work you are about the start. Notice how the student learned to keep his eyes on the cross which resulted in his freedom from impurity. Look forward to hearing similar accounts from your students in the days to come. We are praying for you.

Eamonn Purity Boot Camp testimony:

Eamonn writes, "The Setting Captives Free Purity Boot Camp course has been used by Jesus Christ to set me free from bondage to impurity.

What I've mainly learned is to look at our wonderful Savior Jesus Christ on the cross taking all my punishment, dying for my sin, and rising for my justification and righteousness. I've learned to wash at the cross continually, fellowship with Jesus, walk in the Spirit, and war against my flesh to glorify Christ. I also learned I'm not condemned and that I'm not my sin and that the law of the Spirit of life has set me from the law of sin and death.

The biblical principles taught in this course have changed my life. I've seen the truth about Jesus Christ and the power of His resurrection. I've learned intimacy with the Lord and now love the Lord because I truly believe that He first loved me by dying for me on the cross. I've mainly kept my eyes on the cross, and the 'snakebites' of sin are being eradicated through Christ. I've learned to worship Father God in Christ without fear."

Introduction

*T*his book will function as your guide to hosting group studies using the **Setting Captives Free - Purity Boot Camp** book. It contains the expected answers to the questions in the Purity Boot Camp book, suggested teachings for opening and closing the group sessions, comments, and discussion points.

Participants in your study may use the printed book, the e-book, or the free online version of the Setting Captives Free Purity Boot Camp book. If possible, we suggest the leader sends out a link to the free, online study of the Purity Boot Camp course (https://settingcaptivesfree.com/course/pure30).

Participants who do the study online can check the box to receive an email of their answers for each lesson, and they can then print their answers and bring them to the group study.

Whichever method participants wish to use, they should be encouraged to study through the first five lessons in preparation for the first meeting.

The group study is designed to span six weeks in total, meeting once per week. During each weekly meeting, you will review the answers from the five lessons; therefore, participants should complete five lessons each week before coming to the discussion group. The meetings are designed to last for one hour, but you are free to make them shorter or longer as desired.

We suggest a group size of eight to ten people. If your group is more extensive than this, it would be helpful to break up into smaller groups with a leader/facilitator for each smaller group during the discussion portion of the meeting. We recommend that all leaders study through and complete the Purity Boot Camp course before leading a small group.

You will want to structure the weekly meetings in such a way that encourages everyone to participate, but your role as a leader is to keep the focus of the group on the course material, helping to avoid tangents, distractions, and "rabbit trail" discussions.

Here is a suggested (not obligatory) outline that can be followed in the group meetings:

- Welcome of all students, leader prayer for the meeting: **5 minutes**
- Introductory teaching by the leader: **10 minutes**
- Small group review of five lessons, led by discussion leader: **30 minutes**
- Summary teaching by the leader: **10 minutes**

Total time: approximately 1 hour

We encourage a time of worship through gospel songs each week if able and have suggested worship songs for each meeting. These can be found at the end of the suggested teaching for each week.

First Meeting

- Welcome and greeting of all participants, leader prays for the meeting: **10 minutes**

*W*armly welcome all participants, pray for God's presence, power, and gospel love to be evident, and for all participants to be enlightened, challenged, and encouraged through the study.

- Testimony (if available): **10 minutes**

During this first meeting, it would be helpful if one of the leaders would share their testimony and experience of studying through the lessons in the Setting Captives Free Purity Boot Camp course, to give hope to the participants that gospel change can happen to them, too. This does not have to be long, but should include three main points:

1. **Their previous struggle**
2. **Their experience when studying through the Setting Captives Free Purity Boot Camp course**, including both **spiritual changes** ("I've experienced the love of Jesus and the power of the gospel, etc.") and **changes in their lives and their relationships with others.**
3. **Provide hope to the hearers.** "If God can make these changes in me, I know He can work in you as well," etc.

- Introductory teaching by the leader: **10 minutes**

Let's begin our first teaching session just now, and then we will break up into small groups for a time of discussion and interaction.

Teaching

Welcome again, so good to be with you. I'm excited to study with you for the next six weeks, and today we'll begin our study by turning to the Book of Isaiah chapter 61.

You might recall that Jesus chose this very text from which to preach His first sermon, and after He read what we're about to read He said, "*Today, this Scripture is fulfilled in your hearing*" (Luke 4:21 NIV).

So, let's read it together:

> *Isaiah 61:1-3 (NIV) The Spirit of the Sovereign Lord is on me, because the Lord has anointed me to proclaim good news to the poor. He has sent me to bind up the brokenhearted, to proclaim freedom for the captives and release from darkness for the prisoners, 2 to proclaim the year of the Lord's favor and the day of vengeance of our God, to comfort all who mourn, 3 and provide for those who grieve in Zion—to bestow on them a crown of beauty instead of ashes, the oil of joy instead of mourning, and a garment of praise instead of a spirit of despair. They will be called oaks of righteousness, a planting of the Lord for the display of his splendor.*

So, here we see the main mission of the Messiah, Jesus Christ. He came to proclaim good news (Isaiah 61:1) to poor, brokenhearted captives and prisoners who are in darkness (Isaiah 61:1-2).

Sexual immorality is like a dark prison. It doesn't matter what kind of impurity it is - pornography, self-gratification, illicit sex, etc. - it drags us down and traps us. And once we have become imprisoned by it, we find it is like Alcatraz. It feels inescapable. We can make all the vows or promises we like, but these cannot set us free.

But in Isaiah 61, we see that the work of Jesus Christ is to set us free! Jesus declares in John 8:36, "*if the Son sets you free you will be free indeed.*"

So, what does this tell us? It tells us that we can have real hope for freedom because our freedom will be attributed to the work of Jesus Christ, not our own works. If we had to work off our guilt or somehow measure up to God's standard of perfection, we would have no hope at all, for though our spirit is willing, our flesh is weak (Matthew 26:41). But when we understand that Jesus came to "proclaim freedom for the captives" and to "release prisoners of darkness" then we can have real hope that we too can be free. We cannot break free on our own, but Jesus can set us free. This course is designed to help us experience the work of Jesus and the freedom He offers!

It doesn't matter if we were years in darkness or decades in bondage, the Son came to set us free! And, I'm not talking about living in a halfway house, being in perpetual "recovery," or believing the world's lie: "once an addict, always an addict." I'm talking about being released from our dark prison cells, living in true and lasting freedom.

Jesus sets us free by taking our sin on Himself and dying with it. In this way, He removes the penalty of sin from us. And when the penalty of sin has been removed from us, then the power of sin over us is broken. As Charles Wesley wrote, Jesus "breaks the pow'r of canceled sin; He sets the pris'ner free..."

So, God's Word encourages us today to have hope for real freedom. Not that we will ever be sinless in this life, but that Jesus will free us from life-dominating sin and release us from bondage to sin. He does this through His death in our place, His resurrection from the dead, and by giving us His Holy Spirit to transform us into His image.

I'm praying that as we go through this material together that God will not only set captives free but also unite our hearts in His love.

For now, we are going to break up into small groups to discuss the first five lessons of the book, but when we come back together, we will return to Isaiah 61 and see the results that Jesus has achieved for us.

Let's pray.

Father in heaven, we come to you in prayer asking that you would make the work of Jesus Christ real in our hearts and lives. Thank You for sending Your Son to die on the cross, effectively coming right into our darkness and into our jail cell and opening the door. Lord Jesus, thank you for suffering for us, for dying in our place, for rising to justify us before the Father. Please make our time together fruitful for your glory and our good. In Jesus' name, Amen.

Let's go to our small groups now, and then we will come back together for a few closing thoughts.

End of introductory teaching by the leader.

- **Small group review of five lessons, led by discussion leader: 30 minutes**

Small group leader: be friendly and welcoming to all participants, and let them know that each person is encouraged to interact and provide their comments on the lessons. Encourage all to study at home and come prepared to share their answers and their thoughts, and to write out any questions they might have.

Your objective is to review all five lessons in 30 minutes (unless you have determined already to take more time), which averages out to just six minutes per lesson. This means you will need to be open to questions and discussion, but you will need to keep everyone on point and not allow rabbit trail discussions.

Start at lesson one and provide the correct answers to the multiple choice and fill in the blank questions, then encourage discussion and interaction around the essay questions.

Heart Change

*S*mall group leader: Welcome to the Purity Boot Camp course. I'm looking forward to this study with you and hope that we can learn from each other as we look into God's word together. Let's review the answers to the first five lessons now.

Question 1: How about you? Please describe your struggle here:

Answer: Give each person a short time to introduce themselves.

Our objective here is not to focus on past sins and failures, but rather an acknowledgment of sin's struggles and past power over us. The group leader should not allow this time to degenerate into a confessional, but keep it a friendly introduction and acknowledgment of the common struggle with impurity.

Question 2: What is God's promise as recorded in Ezekiel 36:26-27?
- ☐ He will reward those who try hard to be free.
- ☐ He will honor our commitment to stop sinning.
- ☐ He will give us a new heart and spirit, and motivate us toward obedience.

Answer: He will give us a new heart and spirit, and motivate us toward obedience. This is truly our only hope that God would change our hearts toward impurity, giving us a deep distaste for that which we once found alluring. If God does this, if He changes our hearts, we will be free.

Question 3: Please fill in the blank: "Create in me a _____ _____, O God, and renew a steadfast spirit within me."

Answer: Pure heart.

Question 4: If so, maybe you would like to cry out to God right here, like David did and I did. We will unite in prayer with you.

Answer: Unique to each student. If anyone reads what they have written in crying out to the Lord, it would be good to pause and pray for that person, agreeing in prayer that God will hear, answer and change their hearts.

Question 5: What things do you intend to do, right now, to shut the door to Satan's temptations?

Answer: Here the leader can make the statement that unless we shut the door to pornography and sexual impurity the devil will continue to ransack our lives with it. Offer suggestions and encouragement to those who are struggling in knowing how to shut the door to temptation.

Question 6: What happened to those in the Corinthian church who had previously been sexually immoral (among other things)?
- ☐ They stayed that way, after all, they were born that way and couldn't change.
- ☐ They were washed, set apart, cleansed and justified.
- ☐ They worked hard at changing and decided to be different.

Answer: They were washed, set apart, cleansed and justified.

Question 7: Please share any final thoughts on this first day of your course.

Answer: Answers will vary.

Question 8: What are your thoughts about Garrett's testimony? Please share.

Answer: Allow students the opportunity to share.

Washing at the Cross

Question 1: Are you seeing the need for a heart change and asking God to do it?

Answer: Varies; the desire is that all would desire a heart change.

Question 2: What is it that would cleanse people from impurity and remove idolatry from the land?
- ☐ We are cleansed when we make a covenant with our eyes not to look lustfully at others.
- ☐ We are washed clean by taking steps to make up for the wrongs we've done.
- ☐ A fountain would be opened to cleanse them from sin.

Answer: A fountain would be opened to cleanse them from sin.

Question 3: According to Zechariah 13:1-2, what would happen when God opened a fountain?
- ☐ People would be cleansed from sin and impurity.
- ☐ God would remove idolatry.
- ☐ God would banish the spirit of impurity.
- ☐ All of the above.

Answer: All of the above.

Question 4: Do you want this kind of washing? Share your thoughts.

Answer: Allow for sharing. The leader should be praying and asking God to bring about heart change through washing at the cross of Jesus Christ.

Question 5: Please fill in the blank: "On that day a fountain will be opened... to _____ them from sin and impurity" (Zechariah 13:1).

Answer: Cleanse.

Question 6: What happens to sinners who are "plunged beneath that flood"?
- ☐ They drown.
- ☐ They lose all their guilty stains.
- ☐ They tell others about that fountain.

Answer: They lose all their guilty stains.

Walking by the Spirit

Question 1: In the previous lesson, we talked about the first foundational principle of freedom, do you remember what it is?

☐ Find an accountability partner.

☐ Washing at the cross.

☐ Read your Bible and pray.

Answer: Washing at the cross.

Question 2: Please fill in the blank. If you "walk by the Spirit, you will not _____ the desires of the flesh" (Galatians 5:16).

Answer: Gratify.

Question 3: According to Galatians 5:17, what is the conflict that you and I experience every day as Christians?

☐ To gratify our flesh using porn or to read our Bibles and pray.

☐ The mind against the body.

☐ The flesh against the Spirit.

Answer: The flesh against the Spirit.

Question 4: According to Ephesians 1:13, how do people receive the Holy Spirit?

☐ We receive the Spirit when we believe the gospel message.

☐ We receive the Spirit when we join a church and get baptized.

☐ We receive the Spirit when we start overcoming sin.

Answer: We receive the Spirit when we believe the gospel message.

Question 5: How did the Galatians receive the Spirit of God?

- ☐ By obeying the Law.
- ☐ By trying to overcome sin.
- ☐ By seeing the clearly portrayed message of Christ crucified for their sins and believing that message.

Answer: By seeing the clearly portrayed message of Christ crucified for their sins and believing that message.

Question 6: If you are a believer, please share how you came to faith in Christ. If you are not a believer, what is holding you back? Please share.

Answer: If anyone wants to share here then that is good, but we are not looking for "life stories," but rather testimonies of when they first heard the gospel and put faith in it.

Question 7: What does it mean to you to walk by the Spirit? Please share your thoughts here.

Answer: Walking by the Spirit is to be energized and enabled to leave a life of fleshly gratification and to walk closely with the Lord Jesus.

LESSON 4:

Warring Against the Flesh

Question 1: What are the two foundational principles of freedom that we have studied in the course?
- ☐ Do your best, Do hard work.
- ☐ Keep God's law and Keep in God's Word.
- ☐ Washing at the cross, Walking by the Spirit.

Answer: Washing at the cross, Walking by the Spirit.

Question 2: Please share about your experience in this battle of lust and impurity.

Answer: Teach them that we are not looking for this group to be a confessional, but rather short sharing of personal experiences that are relatable.

Question 3: What time was it when David had this fall to sexual immorality?
- ☐ The time when kings go to bed.
- ☐ The time when kings plant their fields.
- ☐ The time when kings go off to war.

Answer: The time when kings go off to war.

Question 4: From Colossians 2:13-15, list everything that happened at the cross:

Answer: God made us alive with Christ; He forgave us all our sins, having canceled the charge of our legal indebtedness; He disarmed the powers and authorities.

Question 5: Please fill in the blank: "And having disarmed the powers and authorities, he made a public spectacle of them, _____ over them by the _____ ."

Answer: Triumphing; Cross.

Question 6: How did Jesus win at the cross? Share your thoughts.

Answer: Jesus won by laying down His life, by dying to His flesh and living in obedience to the Father. "*My food is to do the will of Him who sent me and to finish His work*" (John 4:34). We win the same way Jesus won - not through *trying* but through *dying*. When we have gazed at the cross of Jesus long enough, we find the same desire within us that Jesus had within Him: to die to our flesh and to live for the will of God. So, *the answer lies in looking at the cross.* Read the following verse and ask your participants to notice on what specifically we are supposed to focus:

> *Hebrews 12:2-3 (NIV) fixing our eyes on Jesus, the pioneer, and perfecter of faith. For the joy set before him, he endured the cross, scorning its shame, and sat down at the right hand of the throne of God. 3 Consider him who endured such opposition from sinners, so that you will not grow weary and lose heart.*

As we focus on Jesus' death in our place, His enduring the cross, His enduring opposition from sinners, we don't grow weary and lose heart, on the contrary, we are awakened and energized to die to our sin and to live for God and serve others.

Question 7: Are you ready? What is your answer, soldier?

Answer: Leaders should understand that some participants will be ready and will want to fight sin to the death. Others will not like this analogy of being a soldier and learning how to fight. And yet that is what we are called to be. If time permits, please read through Ephesians 6:10-20 with your group, helping them to see that believers are to war against their flesh and the devil.

Warring Against the Flesh
God's Battle Plan

Question 1: What are the three foundational principles of freedom?
- ☐ Choose an addiction/recovery group, get a sponsor and attend meetings.
- ☐ Washing at the cross, Walking by the Spirit, Warring against the flesh.
- ☐ Just say no, surrender to the Lord and deny yourself.

Answer: Washing at the cross, Walking by the Spirit, Warring against the flesh.

Question 2: Why do you think it's important to turn to God, to read His Word and to get help from Him?

Answer: God and His power in the gospel, as applied by the Holy Spirit is the only lasting solution available. All step groups and support programs are destined to fail unless they are instilling the gospel of Jesus Christ, which is the power of God, into the hearts of all.

Question 3: What does this loss at Ai teach us?
- ☐ That little sins aren't very important, better to focus on big ones.
- ☐ That we must consult with the Lord and find out from His Word how to be victorious.
- ☐ That when we win one battle, it is proof that we will continue to win.

Answer: That we must consult with the Lord and find out from His Word how to be victorious.

Question 4: Please fill in the blank. "For we have no power to face this vast army that is attacking us. We do not know what to do, but _____ _____ _____ ____ _____" (2 Chronicles 20:12).

Answer: But our eyes are on you.

Question 5: What truths do you see in 2 Chronicles 20:15-17?

Answer: Do not be afraid or discouraged; the battle is God's; take up your position and stand firm; go out and face the battle; the Lord will be with you.

Question 6: Please share your final thoughts on this lesson today:

Answer: Varies.

Thank you for all your answers and comments. Let's move back into our large group study now for the final summary teaching of today.

- Summary teaching by the leader: **10 minutes**

Hello again, everyone, I hope you enjoyed the small group discussion.

Earlier we saw from Isaiah 61 the role of Jesus Christ in coming to release sin-captives and to open the prison doors of those in darkness. As we close today, let's return to Isaiah 61 and rejoice together in seeing the results that Jesus produces as He frees captives.

> *Isaiah 61:4-7 (NIV) They will rebuild the ancient ruins and restore the places long devastated; they will renew the ruined cities that have been devastated for generations. 5 Strangers will shepherd your flocks; foreigners will work your fields and vineyards. 6 And you will be called priests of the Lord, you will be named ministers of our God. You will feed on the wealth of nations, and in their riches you will boast. 7 Instead of your shame you will receive a double portion, and instead of disgrace you will rejoice in your inheritance. And so you will inherit a double portion in your land, and everlasting joy will be yours.*

Notice that when Jesus Christ opens prison doors and sets captives free that those released will rebuild, restore and renew. We see this fulfilled literally when the nation of Israel came back from exile to rebuild Jerusalem, restore the nation and renew their worship of the one true God.

But, spiritually speaking, this happens to us as well. In sin, we destroyed so much, lives were hurt, relationships were damaged; and consequently, we lived in guilt and shame. But when Jesus releases us, there will be much rebuilding and restoring because He enables it. Some relationships can be restored, others will be renewed, and there will be much rebuilding and renewing of true worship that happens in our lives.

Notice the result: "*Instead of disgrace you will rejoice in your inheritance... everlasting joy will be yours!*" Rejoicing and never-ending joy! Oh, friends, if you've experienced the devastation and destruction of impurity, let's believe God's Word that He will set us free and when He does there will be much renewing and rebuilding and restoring going on in our lives.

I say to you today, on the authority of God's Word, no matter how far impurity has taken you, or how long it has kept you, instead of disgrace you will rejoice and instead of shame, everlasting joy will be yours! This happens because of the commitment of Jesus to go clear to the cross to rescue us, even to the grave and back, and the repentance that message produces in our hearts.

Let's close in prayer.

Suggested Songs
There is a Redeemer
Just as I am by Travis Cottrell
Turn Your Eyes upon Jesus by Hillsong

Week 2

- Welcome of all students, leader prayer for the meeting: **5 minutes**
- Introductory teaching by the leader: **10 minutes**

*W*elcome back! This is week two of our study together. Today, I want to share with you how we get trapped in sin, and how we are rescued and delivered from it.

If we go back to the beginning, we see the devil coming to Eve in the form of a crafty snake. He offered her forbidden fruit, and the Bible is very clear as to why she took and ate it:

> *Genesis 3:6 (NIV) When the woman saw that the fruit of the tree was good for food and pleasing to the eye, and also desirable for gaining wisdom, she took some and ate it.*

Notice, Eve "saw" that the tree was good for food, and that it was "pleasing to the eye" and "desirable for gaining wisdom." This is how the devil operates. He dangles something beautiful before our eyes and convince us of its value, as he knows we will then dwell on the image. The image sticks in our minds, the beauty of evil, and it drags us down into the grave when we gratify our flesh with it.

But there is a way to be free from this. First, whenever possible, we need to block all access to forbidden fruit. We must stop hanging around where the tree is if you don't want to eat its fruit. Be serious in developing a plan that removes all access to forbidden fruit.

Now we all know that cutting off access to immoral material is not enough because our minds are full of images that we have previously seen, and any one of them can be recalled and used for fleshly gratification.

The solution to this problem is found in the three principles:

- First, we learn to wash at the cross. In this, we experience not only the forgiveness of our sins but also the cleansing of our hearts and minds. The cross flushes out those immoral memories, washes us clean, and replaces the sinful images with the greater and stronger reality of God's love for us and His power in us.

- Second, at the cross, we are given the Holy Spirit whose role is to walk us away from sin and to Jesus. We are unable to do this on our own, but when the Holy Spirit does it, we experience true freedom!

- Third, we learn to war against our flesh, the world and its sinful offerings, and against the evil one.

So, we need to learn how to wash at the cross, how to walk by the Spirit, and how to war against the flesh; and that is what we are doing in this course. Let's finish our group time by looking at just three verses in Hebrews 12 before we break into small groups:

> *Hebrews 12:1-3 (NIV) Therefore, since we are surrounded by such a great cloud of witnesses, let us throw off everything that hinders and the sin that so easily entangles. And let us run with perseverance the race marked out for us, 2 fixing our eyes on Jesus, the pioneer and perfecter of faith. For the joy set before him, he endured the cross, scorning its shame, and sat down at the right hand of the throne of God. 3 Consider him who endured such opposition from sinners, so that you will not grow weary and lose heart.*

Here we are taught two significant points:

- **Throw off excess weight and run!** Remove access to pornography and throw off anything else that has causes stumbling in your life; you will not only feel lighter, but you will also be able to run your Christian race unhindered.

- **Fix your eyes on Jesus.** Glue your eyes to Him. Become preoccupied with Him. Learn to look away from your sin, your failures, your past, and your pain and instead fixate on Christ. Paul said, *"Brothers and sisters, I do not consider myself yet to have taken hold of it. But one thing*

I do: Forgetting what is behind and straining toward what is ahead..." (Philippians 3:13).

After we meet in our small groups to discuss this past week's lessons, we will come back together and see what specifically we are to focus on when we "fix our eyes on Jesus." Let's close in prayer.

Let's break into small groups now for our study:

- Small group review of five lessons, led by discussion leader: **30 minutes**

Warring Against the Flesh
Learn to Fight!

Question 1: Are you aware that you are at war, and that you are responsible for learning how to fight to win? What are your thoughts?

Answer: Sometimes, we can develop an unbalanced view of Christian life. We get so caught up resting in the finished work of Christ, enjoying all the blessings, celebrating God's love, and giving thanks for salvation that we forget about other important aspects of our faith.

The Christian life is also warfare, and we are soldiers of the cross! We don't fight other people (our battle is not against flesh and blood); but we are called to war against our flesh, the powers of darkness, all deception, and the attacks of Satan.

Those who will not acknowledge the Christian life as a battle are deceiving themselves and will remain captive under the power of the evil one, prisoners of their flesh, and in bondage to their cravings.

The church as a whole needs to wake up and learn warfare (Judges 3:2)!

Question 2: How does Romans 8:13 show us that we are in a life and death struggle?
- ☐ If we live gratifying our flesh, we die, but if we put to death the flesh we live. It's life or death.
- ☐ If we don't put on our armor, then we will die, but if we fight in the Lord's army, then we will live.
- ☐ If we don't go to our group meetings, then we will die, but if we are accountable to a lot of people, then we will live.

Answer: If we live gratifying our flesh, we die, but if we put to death the flesh we live. It's life or death.

Question 3: Do you see the importance of developing your plan to war against your flesh?

☐ Yes, a lot!
☐ Somewhat.
☐ Not really.

Answer: "Yes, a lot!" is the desired answer, but some students may answer differently. This is a good place to remind everyone of the absolute necessity for all people to seek God for help. Only God can raise the dead, open the eyes of the blind, change the heart of sinful man, and stir in us a holy passion to fight and kill that which wants to kill us. Only God can stir up a holy fire within us that will burn away all sin and impurity. Only God can make us hate what we once loved and love what we once hated. Only God can make us say from the bottom of our hearts, "Yes, I'm sick and tired of losing; I want to fight and to start winning! A Lot!

Question 4: Please consider your own life and sin struggles. Where have you been falling? Please be as specific as possible in your answer:

Answer: It would help if you, as the group leader, would share areas in which you have fallen in the past; otherwise participants might not want to share their more recent struggles.

Question 5: What is your battle plan to crucify your lusts? Be willing to be extreme in this; it's life or death!

Answer: Again you, as the leader can share the plans that you have implemented in your own life, as encouragement for all to share.

Washing at the Cross
The Cross Cleanses Us

Question 1: Are you seeking the Lord for a heart change? Please share:

Answer: Theologically, we receive a new heart, a new spirit, and a new life at the new birth (Ezekiel 36:25-27). Practically, God must turn our hearts away from impurity and to the cross by the power of the Spirit. Again, only God can do this; no human can. Encourage all participants to seek the Lord earnestly to change their hearts truly, or they will continue to live under the power of darkness as prisoners of their flesh.

Question 2: According to Ephesians 5:25-27, what is the evidence of Christ's love for you?
- ☐ He said, "I love you!"
- ☐ He gave Himself up for you, dying on a cross.
- ☐ He loved you by giving you the Bible.

Answer: He gave Himself up for you, dying on a cross.

Question 3: According to Ephesians 5:26, what is the stated purpose that Jesus gave Himself for us? Please fill in the blanks: Christ loved the church and gave himself up for her to make her holy, _____ her by the _____ with water through the word.

Answer: Cleansing; washing.

Question 4: According to Ephesians 5:27, what did the cross of Jesus Christ make you (as a believer in Jesus)?
- ☐ Radiant.
- ☐ Without any sin stains whatsoever.
- ☐ Straightened all wrinkles.
- ☐ Removed all blemishes.
- ☐ Holy and pure.
- ☐ All of the above.

Answer: All of the above. It is critical to focus on the cross, to continually display the power of it and the glory of it. To look at all that happened there, to experience it anew daily, to live and fight in the shadow of the cross.

Question 5: What did you learn in this lesson and how will you apply it in your life?

Answer: Try to draw out of participants their thoughts on the power and love of the cross, asking questions about what it means to them and how they experience it daily.

Walking by the Spirit
Hearing the Message of the Cross

Question 1: We remember that the first foundational principle of freedom is Washing at the cross. What is the second principle?
- ☐ Promise to stop viewing pornography.
- ☐ Commit to your spouse to be pure.
- ☐ Walking by the Spirit.

Answer: Walking by the Spirit.

Question 2: What do you think it would look like, in your own life, to be empowered by the Spirit of God rather than the flesh? Please be specific:

Answer: Answers will vary.

Question 3: According to Galatians 3:1-5, when does a person receive the Holy Spirit and experience His miraculous presence?
- ☐ By believing the message that Christ was crucified.
- ☐ When we submit to the law and begin to obey it.
- ☐ When we change from being an atheist to having faith in God.
- ☐ When we work at overcoming all impurity.

Answer: By believing the message that Christ was crucified.

Question 4: According to 1 Corinthians 2:2, to what was Paul's message limited?

Answer: This is not to say that Paul never spoke of any other subject to the Corinthians; but rather, that the death of Jesus on the cross and His resurrection three days later were at the heart of it all. The gospel is the most important message. Every sin and difficulty of life can and should be seen in the light of the good news of Christ crucified and risen. At the cross, the power of the Holy Spirit is active and lives are transformed, and this is what we want.

Question 5: According to 1 Corinthians 2:4-5, with what was Paul's message accompanied?
- ☐ Good oratory skills.
- ☐ The Spirit's power.
- ☐ Worldly wisdom.

Answer: The Spirit's power.

Question 6: In 1 Corinthians 10:3-4, the Bible tells us that this rock was Christ. How can you see the gospel in Exodus 17:1-6?

Answer: "That Rock was Christ," so Christ was struck on the cross and out poured the Holy Spirit as a river of living water. It's the Holy Spirit, who flows from the cross, that quenches our thirst and satisfies our longings. It's the Holy Spirit who walks us away from fleshly living and selfish gratifying. The cross and the Spirit are intimately connected so that we receive the Spirit at the cross, and we continue to drink of Him as He flows from the crucified/risen Savior.

Question 7: Please state what you learned from this lesson today:

Answer: Varies.

Warring Against Our Flesh
Fighting in the Shadow of the Cross

Question 1: What does it mean to you personally that the Lord is going to bring you out of Egypt, set you free, lift your head and make you smile again?

Answer: Most of the time, people long in bondage to impurity have had all the hope beat out of them. They've tried on their own to get free and have failed much and often, and now, they can only hang their head in hopeless shame. But Jesus sets captives free! That's the whole purpose of His coming to this earth, living a perfect life in our place, dying on the cross to save us and set us free, and rising from the dead to justify us (Romans 4:25).

Question 2: How is the implementation of your battle plan? Is there anything that needs to change in it? Please share:

Answer: If students are still falling to sexual impurity, they must learn to adjust their plan, close the gaps in their armor, do something different. Don't let participants use the excuse, "But my situation is unique." Yes, we're all unique, but God gives specific plans to each one of us for our unique situation, and He enables us to fight to win!

Question 3: What differences do you see between fighting under the shadow of the cross and fighting in your own strength?

Answer: Answers will vary.

Question 4: When the Amalekites attacked Israel what did Moses do to ensure victory for the Israelites?

- ☐ He brought out the Law to read to the people and told them to obey.
- ☐ He and two others went up on a hill and stood there with his arms up.
- ☐ He put on his armor and led by marching the people into battle.

Answer: He and two others went up on a hill and stood there with his arms up.

Question 5: Do you see that God made the outcome of this battle dependent on what the man in the middle did? Please fill in the blank. "As long as Moses held up his _____, the Israelites were _____."

Answer: Hands; winning. Like this story in Exodus 17, God made the outcome of our battle with sin totally dependent upon what Jesus did on the cross. There He fought Satan and won (Colossians 2:15), there He removed God's wrath from all who believe (1 Thessalonians 1:10), there He rescued us from the power of darkness (Colossians 1:13), there He reconciled us to God (Romans 5:10), there He redeemed us from our empty way of life (1 Peter 1:18)! Jesus won through dying, and all believers win our battles the same way because the cross crucifies the world to us and us to the world (Galatians 6:14).

Question 6: What did you learn in this lesson today and how will you apply it?

Answer: Answers will vary.

Washing at the Cross
Gospel Cleansing

Question 1: What are the three foundational principles of freedom given in this course?
- ☐ Decide to follow Christ, obey God's Word, stop viewing porn.
- ☐ Washing at the cross, Walking by the Spirit, Warring against the flesh.
- ☐ Listening to Jesus, learning of Jesus, following Jesus.

Answer: Washing at the cross, Walking by the Spirit, Warring against the flesh.

Question 2: Can you relate to this description? What was it like for you personally?

Answer: We want all participants to share, but be very careful about letting this time degenerate into a self-focused venting about their sinful life and the sharing of impure details.

You as the leader must take to heart Ephesians 5:11-12, "*Have nothing to do with the fruitless deeds of darkness, but rather expose them. 12 It is shameful even to mention what the disobedient do in secret.*"

You will notice in the Purity Boot Camp material that I do not ever discuss the details of my past sin for this would be "shameful." All we are looking for from the participants in this question is a general acknowledgment that yes, sin is captivity, sin is bondage, and we were all enslaved to it at one time.

Question 3: John 13:1 shows the motivation of Jesus Christ for doing what is about to follow in this chapter. What was His motivation? Please fill in the blank: Having _____ his own who were in the world, he _____ them to the end.

Answer: Loved; loved.

Question 4: What was Jesus' response to Peter? "Unless I wash you, you have _____ _____ with me" (John 13:8).

Answer: No part.

Question 5: According to John 13:9, how did Jesus' declaration affect Peter?

Answer: Peter was filled with longing for Jesus and to be washed completely by Him: "not just my feet but my hands and my head as well!"

Question 6: Would you like to pray as Peter did? Please take this space to write out your prayer to Jesus.

Answer: Ask if anyone would share their prayer. Not necessary.

Question 7: Please share how this story in John 13 reveals the cross of Jesus Christ to you:

Answer: This great act of service that Jesus did in washing the disciples' feet, pales in comparison to His greater act of service in dying on the cross to wash us internally. In Jesus' statement, *"unless I wash you, you have no part with me"* (John 13:8) shows the need we have to wash at the cross.

Question 8: What are your thoughts about Ken's testimony? Please share here:

Answer: Allow students to share.

Summary teaching by the leader: **10 minutes**

Welcome back, everyone. I hope you enjoyed the discussion and study. We started this session today looking at Hebrews 12:1-3 and seeing that we must learn how to "fix our eyes on Jesus."

Now, let's consider our focal point according to the text. Is it Jesus' miraculous birth? His perfect life? His miracles? His teachings?

Yes, those things are all important, but in Hebrews 12, we are explicitly told to see Jesus going to the cross and dying in our place. We are told this twice: once in Hebrews 12:2 and again in verse 3.

> *Hebrews 12:2 (NIV) fixing our eyes on Jesus, the pioneer, and perfecter of faith. For the joy set before him, he endured the cross, scorning its shame, and sat down at the right hand of the throne of God.*

This tells us that Jesus had joy as He endured the cross. This joy was in obeying His Father and finishing His work. The joy was in saving you and setting you free.

And this is what we are to "fix our eyes on." As we look to the cross, we see that Jesus died to His flesh; and we are called and equipped to die to our flesh too. As we look to the cross, we see Jesus had joy in His cross-work, and we are taught that we can happily die to sin with Him.

This is the opposite of the world's method of working the program, white knuckling it, and feeling angry and frustrated during the process. No, believers die with joy! We put both arms around the cross and die grateful and happy!

And in Hebrews 12:3, we see the same exhortation to focus on the cross, as it tells us to "consider him who endured such opposition from sinners so that you will not grow weary and lose heart." Focusing on and considering Christ in His substitutional death on the cross energizes us, fills us with love, and helps us to take up our own cross. As we consider Him enduring opposition from sinners, we will not grow weary in warring against our own flesh, and we will not give in to depression and discouragement. We will not "lose heart."

We started this session showing how Eve "saw" the forbidden fruit of the tree of knowledge of good and evil, and that it was "pleasing to her eye." We acknowledged that Satan wants to put something beautiful before our eyes to lure us into sin.

But now, in closing, we are reminded that we can have our entire eyesight taken up with a different tree - the tree of the cross. For Adam and Eve's focus on the wrong tree led to sin and death to the whole human race, but Jesus went to the tree (cross) to redeem us and set us free from sin and disobedience. *"Consequently, just as one trespass resulted in condemnation for all people, so also one righteous act resulted in justification and life for all people. For just as through the disobedience of the one man the many were made sinners, so also through the obedience of the one man the many will be made righteous"* (Romans 5:18-19).

We are now called to look at Jesus enduring the cross for us, watch as He joyfully suffers in our place, and have that view eclipse everything else in our lives. Let's fix our eyes on Jesus, who for the joy set before Him endured the cross, and sat down at the right hand of God.

Summary: the gospel is not "the basics," but rather the main point! It's the most important point (1 Corinthians 15:1-5)! It's not the "ABC's of Christianity," it is the "A Through Z," and we are told to fix our eyes on Jesus and the gospel! Let's close in prayer.

Suggested Songs
Amazing Grace
In Christ Alone by Keith Getty
Sinless Savior by Aaron Keyes.

Week 3

- Welcome of all students, leader prayer for the meeting: **5 minutes**
- Introductory teaching by the leader: **10 minutes**

*G*reetings everyone, so glad to be back with you this week. Before we separate into small groups, let's take a moment to consider what is most important. In the context of our current study, taking a stand on what is most important sets us free, strengthens us, stabilizes us, makes us fruitful in ministry and productive in our lives.

So, let's look at God's Word to see what is most important. Look with me at 1 Corinthians 15. In this session, we will look at verses 1 and 2, and in our closing session, we will look at verses 3 through 6.

> *1 Corinthians 15:1-2 (NIV) Now, brothers and sisters, I want to remind you of the gospel I preached to you, which you received and on which you have taken your stand. 2 By this gospel you are saved, if you hold firmly to the word I preached to you. Otherwise, you have believed in vain.*

In verse 3, Paul tells us the gospel is that which is "of first importance." The gospel is the main point of all of Scripture, both the Old and New Testament. The gospel is what saves us and sets us free, when we believe it and hold to it.

Notice that the Corinthians had first received the gospel, and second, had taken their stand on the gospel. They had heard the good news that Christ had died for their sins, thereby releasing them from the guilt and penalty of sin, and they received this good news. They believed and embraced it wholeheartedly. We must do this too if we would live in freedom.

But believing is sometimes easier said than done. By natural reasoning, our sin looms large in our minds and threatens to keep us out of God's presence. But we must not forget that God's ways are higher than ours. Through Christ's death and resurrection, God has made a way for the banished to be restored (2 Samuel 14:14). When doubts and fears flood your mind, *bring them to the cross.* Finish your sentence!

Look to the cross and see that Christ assumed your guilt and removed your sin, dying under the penalty of it to free you from it. Remember that Jesus took the full brunt of the wrath of God so that there is none left for you!

Recall that Christ gave you His righteousness. God receives you because, through faith in Jesus, you are as righteous as Christ Himself.

Push past your sins, cast off your doubts and fears, and embrace the good news as a gift purchased by Jesus specifically for you. Ask God to open your heart and give you faith to receive the gospel of Jesus Christ.

The Corinthians not only received the gospel, but they also took their stand on it. They planted their flag on the gospel. They declared the gospel to be the truth for which they would live, and the only hill on which they would die. The circumstances of life were viewed from the vantage point of the gospel. This is what it means to take a stand on the gospel.

And this, friends, is what not only frees us but also stabilizes us. Taking a stand on the gospel keeps us from alternating between gorging ourselves on lust and impurity one day and being hyper-religious and overzealous the next. Paul writes:

> *Romans 16:25 (NIV) Now to him who is able to **establish you** in accordance with my gospel, the message I proclaim about Jesus Christ, in keeping with the revelation of the mystery hidden for long ages past,*

The gospel establishes us, stabilizes us, plants our feet firmly in the solid ground of truth, keeps us steadfast and immovable. This is the role of the gospel in the life of a believer.

Think of the plethora of platforms on which we might take our stand in life: family values, the sanctity of life, political positions or parties, theological positions or beliefs, anti-drug or alcohol movements, the importance of Bible study, the necessity of prayer, etc.

And while all these issues are of value and have their place, there is only one thing in life that is the *most important* thing, only one thing that should be the object of our intense study and devotion, and that is the gospel of Jesus

Christ. The Corinthians took their stand on the gospel, will you? The Corinthians planted their flag and stood their ground in the gospel, will you?

Friends, there is only one thing that will make you able to live a life and die a death glorifying to God, and that is the gospel of Jesus Christ. For in the gospel, we are safe in the knowledge that Jesus lived for us and died for us. We know that He will not abandon us now. When we consider how Jesus suffered, died and rose for us, we are empowered to endure suffering and to trust in Him for deliverance. As we contemplate Jesus' sacrificial love for us, His love compels us to live in accordance with the Scriptures not gratifying our lusts but instead, putting sin to death so that we can live as the righteous people Christ has made us to be.

Let's make the most important thing in Scripture - the gospel - to be the most important thing in our lives!

Let's break into our small groups now.

- **Small group review of five lessons, led by discussion leader: 30 minutes**

Walking by the Spirit
Overcoming the Flesh

Question 1: Do you identify with the above description? If so, how?

Answer: Answer varies by student.

Question 2: According to Psalm 107:13-16 above, what things did the Lord do for the people who cried out to Him? Please list as many as you see:

Answer: He saved them from their distress; He brought them out of darkness; He broke away their chains; He gave unfailing love; He performed wonderful deeds for mankind; He broke down gates of bronze; He cut through bars of iron.

It is important to acknowledge that God is doing the work here, not man. Man is not taking steps to correct his problem. He is not "working the program" by attending meetings. No, at the cross God saves man. At the cross, God rescues man from darkness. At the cross, God breaks iron chains. At the cross, God gives His unfailing love to undeserving sinners. At the cross, God performed a wonderful deed for mankind. At the cross, God broke down gates of bronze with the blood of His own Son. At the cross, God cut through bars of iron to release prisoners.

Question 3: According to Galatians 5:13, what were you called to be?
- ☐ I was called to be perpetually in recovery.
- ☐ I was called to accept that I cannot be free.
- ☐ I was called to be free!

Answer: I was called to be free!

Question 4: According to Galatians 5:13, what are we not to use our freedom to do? "But do not use your freedom to _____ _____ _____ ; rather serve one another in love."

Answer: Indulge the flesh.

Question 5: According to Galatians 5:17, what conflict is every believer experiencing?
- ☐ The heart vs. the mind.
- ☐ The body vs. the spirit.
- ☐ The flesh vs. the spirit.

Answer: The flesh vs. the spirit.

Question 6: If you are led by the Spirit, you are not under the _____.

Answer: Law.

Question 7: According to all that you have learned so far, what makes the difference between living like Galatians 5:19-21 and living like Galatians 5:22-26?

Answer: We are learning to walk by the Spirit.

Question 8: What did you learn in this lesson today, and how will you implement it into your life? Please share.

Answer: Might be different for each student.

Warring Against the Flesh
Overcoming by the Word

Question 1: What are your thoughts about learning how to fight this battle so as to win?

Answer: This is unique to the student, but the hope is to see God develop within each student a passion for putting to death the lusts of their flesh. As we look to the cross, we see Jesus' passion for dying so that sin and death might be destroyed, Satan defeated, and eternal life secured for all who believe. This same passion comes into the heart of each believer as the Holy Spirit works in us, and this passion empowers us to fight against our own flesh and the devil by dying to our former life of sin.

Question 2: What is your current level of hunger for and intake of God's Word?

Answer: Each student has different hunger levels, but help all to understand that immersing ourselves in God's Word is what renews our minds (Romans 12:2) and transforms us. God's Word changes us from one form (defeated in impurity) to another form (victorious in purity).

Question 3: Where would you say you are currently in the spiritual maturity stages listed in 1 John 2:12-14?

Answer: Allow students to share if willing.

Question 4: In 1 John 2:12, what do the "little children" know?
- ☐ They know their sins are forgiven.
- ☐ They don't know much about God.
- ☐ They know how to walk.

Answer: They know their sins are forgiven.

Question 5: In 1 John 2:13, what is said about young men?

Answer: Young men are strong and have overcome the evil one.

Question 6: In 1 John 2:14, what is said about fathers?
- ☐ They are too old to fight anymore.
- ☐ They are characterized by their relationship with God.
- ☐ They are out of touch and irrelevant.

Answer: They are characterized by their relationship with God.

Question 7: According to 1 John 2:14, why are young men strong and over-coming the evil one?

Answer: The answer is, "the Word of God lives in you." The Word of God lives in us, energizes us, empowers us. It makes us like David who "ran into the battle" (1 Samuel 17:48) and slew Goliath. There was no hesitation or fear, only holy boldness to fight and win. This is what God puts in us as we seek Him in His Word. "*But the people that do know their God shall be strong and do exploits*" (Daniel 11:32 KJV).

Question 8: Please list all that is said about the people in 1 Thessalonians 2:13:

Answer: The people in Thessalonica had 1) heard the word of God from Paul and his companions, 2) received the Word of God - they believed it and received Christ, 3) they viewed the gospel properly as being God's Word, not man's word and 4) they began to experience the powerful working of God's word in their hearts and lives.

Question 9: What did you learn in this lesson and how will you apply it?

Answer: Encourage students to share.

Warring Against the Flesh
Overcoming by the Word

Question 1: What were some of the widespread effects of your own involvement with impurity?

Answer: Make sure to keep the group from descending into a confessional where they dump out their impure garbage on everyone in the group. We do not want to hear details, but rather acknowledgments of the destruction and devastation that sin always causes.

Question 2: In Jeremiah 33:7-8, what main concepts are connected together?
- ☐ Captives would be set free; they would be cleansed, forgiven and restored.
- ☐ God would unite Judah and Israel together.
- ☐ Sin and rebellion are connected together.

Answer: Captives would be set free, they would be cleansed, forgiven and restored.

Question 3: In Hebrews 9:13, what did the blood of bulls and goats do for the people?

Answer: The blood of bulls and goats was to cleanse and sanctify, but the Old Testament sacrifices could not change the heart or cleanse the conscience. The sacrifices affected the people externally, cleansing only the body in the form of a ritual.

Question 4: According to Hebrews 9:11-14, to what did the blood of bulls and goats point forward?

- ☐ The hard works (blood, sweat, and tears) we would do to be rid of habitual sin.
- ☐ The blood of Jesus, meaning His sacrificial death.
- ☐ There is always a need to have animals available to sacrifice.

Answer: The blood of Jesus, meaning His sacrificial death.

Question 5: Please fill in the blank: "How much more, then, will the blood of Christ, who through the eternal Spirit offered himself unblemished to God, _____ _____ _____ from acts that lead to death…"

Answer: Cleanse our consciences.

Question 6: Now it is your turn. Please take a moment and write out troubling thoughts you've had and then finish your sentence with the gospel truth.

Answer: This is a very important exercise, teaching the need to disconnect our consciences from captivity to sin and tie them to the blood of Jesus instead. Allow participants adequate time to engage in this exercise; for in it, they learn to preach the gospel to themselves. Stress the need to "finish their sentences" with gospel truth. This is how we "*overcome him by the blood of the Lamb and the word of their testimony*" (Revelation 12:11).

Question 7: According to Hebrews 9:15 why did Jesus die as a ransom?

Answer: Jesus died to pay for the release of the captive. If the ransom price has been paid the captive has been set free.

Question 8: What did you learn in this lesson today?

Answer: Allow all to share.

LESSON 14:

Washing at the Cross
Finding Our Identity in Christ

Question 1: What are the three foundational principles of freedom that we are looking at in this course?
- ☐ Reading the Bible, Repeating Scripture, Running to Prayer.
- ☐ Getting a sponsor, Getting into a program, Going to meetings.
- ☐ Washing at the cross, Walking by the Spirit, Warring against the flesh.

Answer: Washing at the cross, Walking by the Spirit, Warring against the flesh.

Question 2: Have you associated your identity with a particular sin struggle in the past?

Answer: Stress that the world wants us to find our identity in our sin, whereas believers find our identity in Christ. We are children of God purchased by the Son who walk by the Spirit. We do not accept the labels of the world nor receive the identity of our culture.

When Daniel, Hananiah, Mishael, and Azariah were taken captive to Babylon, they were given new names, clothing, and food by their captors. The objective was to strip them of their identity so that they would assume the attitudes and behaviors of their captors and worship the gods of the Babylonians.

Our culture attempts the same thing with Christians today. They place labels on us, try to get us to find our identity in our temptations, and generally attempt to fit us into their mold so that we would worship the god of this world.

Believers stand with Daniel, Hananiah, Mishael, and Azariah, keeping our identity as citizens of another kingdom, believers who died with Christ and rose to new life.

It is critical to teach all participants the need to refuse the language of the culture: we forsake all references to "addiction" and "recovery," to being "triggered" and finding sobriety," etc. These words are subtle changes of biblical truth; the end design is to enslave us. It is imperative that you, as the leader, do not use worldly or psychological terms, but instead use biblical terminology. See Appendix A of the Purity Boot Camp book for further explanation.

Question 3: According to Titus 2: 11-12, what does God's grace do for the believer?
- ☐ Teaches us to deny our worldly passions and live self-controlled lives.
- ☐ Lets us continue to sin knowing that we're always forgiven.
- ☐ Helps us to know that we have been made right with God at the cross so how we live is not important.

Answer: Teaches us to deny our worldly passions and live self-controlled lives.

Question 4: In Romans 6:2, what argument does Paul use to correct this misunderstanding of grace?
- ☐ He says that grace helps us forgive ourselves when we sin.
- ☐ He says that we can keep sinning because grace covers it all.
- ☐ He says that we cannot continue to sin because we died to it.

Answer: He says that we cannot continue to sin because we died to it.

Question 5: What does that sign above Jesus' head say for you?

Answer: What we want participants to see here is that their old life died with Christ. Their past identity is dead; their previous labels have been removed. They are now new creatures in Christ with a new identity and a new life.

Question 6: According to Romans 6:3-4, please list all the things that have happened to you as a believer.

Answer: We were united with Christ in His death, His burial, and His resurrection.

Question 7: According to Romans 6:4, what is the result of our being united with Christ in His death and resurrection?
- ☐ We will never sin again.
- ☐ We are free to sin now that we are saved by grace.
- ☐ We too may live a new life.

Answer: We too may live a new life. Again we want to extract people from captivity to worldly labels and worldly language.

Question 8: What does it mean to you personally to know that you are justified, pardoned and released?

Answer: Allow people to exult in the love of God, the freedom purchased for them by Christ.

Question 9: According to Romans 6:9, what has no mastery over Christ?
- ☐ The Romans.
- ☐ The soldiers guarding His tomb.
- ☐ Death.

Answer: Death.

Question 10: What did you learn in this lesson and how will you apply it?

Answer: Unique to each student.

Warring Against the Flesh
You Are Not Your Sin

Question 1: Do you identify with the opening statement about knowing what to do but struggling to do it? Please share your thoughts:

Answer: Romans 7 is the shared experience of all believers, the point of the passage being that we do not find our identity in our sin. *"It is not I who do it, but sin living in me"* (Romans 7:17).

Question 2: What is Paul's title for himself in Romans 7:14?
- ☐ Saint of God.
- ☐ Slave to sin.
- ☐ Preacher of the gospel.

Answer: Slave to sin.

Question 3: Who was doing the "evil" in Romans 7:18-20?
- ☐ Sin living in Paul.
- ☐ Paul himself.
- ☐ Paul's evil twin.

Answer: Sin living in Paul.

Question 4: Why do you think it is important to not find our identity in sin? Share your thoughts:

Answer: Finding our identity in our temptations or our sin keeps us trapped in it. We will continue to sin because we believe the world's lie that our sin is who we are. But we must come to embrace the truth that "who we are" died with Jesus, that "who we are" was buried in a tomb. Now, it is no longer "who we are" but rather who we *were*. The old impure captive was crucified with Christ and no longer lives (Galatians 2:20). Finding our identity in our temptations keeps us enslaved; but finding our identity in Christ frees us.

Question 5: What is the solution to this "waging war within"?
- ☐ Try harder!
- ☐ Give up!
- ☐ Jesus Christ!

Answer: Jesus Christ!

Question 6: What did you learn from this lesson today?

Answer: Varies by the student.

Question 7: What are your thoughts about Dontaye's testimony? Can you relate to his story? Please share.

Answer: Allow students to share if time permits.

Summary teaching by the leader: 10 minutes

Welcome back!

We began our time by showing that the Corinthians received the gospel of Jesus Christ, and they took their stand on it.

Sadly, over the years, the term gospel has been abused and applied to many things that are not the gospel. People might say the gospel is God's love, all of Jesus' teachings, that we get to go to heaven because of Christ, or so many other "non-gospel" gospels.

But, if we are going to take our stand on the gospel, we must be able to define the gospel. Let's turn to 1 Corinthians 15:3-6 to find the definition of THE gospel:

> *1 Corinthians 15:3-6 (NIV) For what I received I passed on to you as of first importance: that Christ died for our sins according to the Scriptures, 4 that he was buried, that he was raised on the third day according to the Scriptures, 5 and that he appeared to Cephas, and then to the Twelve. 6 After that, he appeared to more than five hundred of the brothers and sisters at the same time, most of whom are still living, though some have fallen asleep.*

Here Paul shows us that the gospel has **two points;** each one of them is followed by a confirming proof.

- **The first point is that Christ died for our sins**, according to the Scriptures. This is followed by the confirming proof that He was buried.

- **The second point is that Christ was raised from the dead** on the third day, according to the Scriptures. The confirming proof is that he was seen by many people, most of whom were still alive in Paul's day and could refute what Paul said if it were not true. "*After his suffering, he presented himself to them and gave many convincing proofs that he was alive. He appeared to them over a period of forty days and spoke about the kingdom of God*" (Acts 1:3 NIV).

So, there we have it: the real gospel! The gospel is the death of Christ for our sins and the resurrection of Christ from the dead on the third day. This message, if truly believed, saves us and sets us free. This message is what we are to receive and on which we take our stand. It's what we are to be known.

And did you notice how each point was "according to the Scriptures?" Paul is referring to the Old Testament Scriptures. If we look carefully at the Old Testament, we can see that God was telling us the gospel story over and over from the very beginning.

In Genesis 1, the earth was empty, in darkness and buried in the deep abyss, the dark grave of water. But on the third day, the waters were separated, the earth was raised out of its watery grave and began producing fruit! Similarly, Jesus emptied Himself unto death, having entered the darkness to rescue us, and was buried in a tomb. But, on the third day, He was raised to life and began producing the fruit of people who would believe this good news and live forever.

In Genesis 2, Adam was put into a deep sleep and had his side opened that He might have a bride. In like fashion, the last Adam, Jesus Christ was put into the deep sleep of death and had His side opened on the cross that you might be His bride through the forgiveness of your sins.

In Genesis 22, Abraham obeyed God and took his son, Isaac, on a three-day journey to a particular mountain. The father laid the wood on the back of his son, the same wood on which the son was to die; and he carried the wood up the hill while Abraham, the father, carried the fire. God stops the sacrifice, and the father receives his son back, "as from the dead" (Hebrews 11:19), on the third day.

In Genesis chapters 37 through 50, we read of Joseph, a son who is loved by his father but hated by his brothers. The brothers sell him into the hands of "gentiles" for pieces of silver, and later in prison, he is falsely accused and placed between two criminals. To one criminal, he brings a message of life, and to the other, a message of death. He is then raised up out of the pit and exalted to the right hand of Pharaoh where he becomes lord of all and gives life to all who come to him. As we look to the cross, we hear Jesus saying to us what Joseph said to his brothers, *"you meant it for evil, but God meant it for good, to accomplish the saving of many lives" (Genesis 50:20).*

And these are only a few of the pictures of the gospel given to us in one book of the Bible. But even with this small sampling, we can see that God's most important message to us is the gospel of Jesus Christ. He has given it to us in hundreds of ways so that we can see it, receive it and take our stand on it.

Paul says, "*For what I received I passed on to you as of first importance: that Christ died for our sins **according to the Scriptures**, 4 that he was buried, that he was raised on the third day **according to the Scriptures**,*" (1 Corinthians 15:3-4).

Close in Prayer.

Suggested Songs
The Wonderful Cross
The Lord is My Salvation by Keith and Kristyn Getty
Christ Lives in Me by Rend Collective.

Week 4

- **Welcome of all students, leader prayer for the meeting: 5 minutes**
- **Introductory teaching by the leader: 10 minutes**

*H*ello friends and welcome to our group study. For our group teaching session today, let's turn to John chapter 4. In this chapter, we read about a woman who has gone from one husband to another; she has had five husbands and is now living with a sixth man to whom she is not married.

Jesus meets her at a well, Jacob's well, and the first thing He does is ask the woman for a drink of water. His request shocks the woman because historically, Jews and Samaritans did not associate; even more, men of character did not speak to women like her.

But Jesus tells her in verse 10, *"If you knew the gift of God and who it is that asks you for a drink, you would have asked him, and he would have given you living water."*

Jesus is speaking of "living water" which we will see later is a reference to "spiritual water," water that quenches the heart and soul, not the body and flesh, but this woman is only able to think in the natural not the spiritual. So, she tells Jesus that the well is deep; and He doesn't have anything with which to draw the water out.

Then Jesus makes an interesting statement which if understood can be life changing for us. Jesus said:

> *John 4:13-14 (NIV) "Everyone who drinks this water will be thirsty again, 14 but whoever drinks the water I give them will never thirst. Indeed, the water I give them will become in them a spring of water welling up to eternal life."*

On the surface, it seems like Jesus is stating the obvious: *"Everyone who drinks this water will be thirsty again."* But He goes on to make a comparison between the water in Jacob's well and the soul quenching water that only He can give.

Drinking physical water provides temporary relief of our thirst, but spiritual water from Christ is eternal and reaches the soul. Only Jesus can quench the thirst of our heart and soul. When we drink the water He gives, it so thoroughly satisfies us and refreshes us so much that we want to share it with others; it becomes in us a source of refreshment to others, a spring of water flowing out of us (John 7:38).

Naturally, the woman becomes very curious about the living water and says in verse 15, "*Sir, give me this water so that I won't get thirsty and have to keep coming here to draw water.*"

Even though she doesn't yet understand, this woman asks for something that we all want. She asks for the living water. We all want eternal satisfaction.

But there is a heart issue that must be addressed before anyone can drink living water. It is the issue of sin. And to address this issue, Jesus says to the woman in verse 16, "*Go, call your husband and come back.*"

This prompts the woman to admit that she has no husband, but she fails to mention her five previous husbands and the man with whom she is currently living. She's ashamed.

Now, we have come to the heart of our teaching. Jesus is making an important connection for this woman. Her ongoing physical thirst is a metaphor for her immoral life.

Jesus said, "*Everyone who drinks this water will thirst again*" and then He asks about her husband to make the connection for her. This woman has gone from one man to another five times; and now, she isn't even bothering with the convention of marriage, she's just living with her lover. Jesus is helping her understand that she is continually "drinking" from a "well" that does not satisfy. What she needs is to drink the "water" Jesus gives, the water that satisfies eternally.

Oh, friends, we can relate to this woman, can't we? It all begins with a desire for sexual satisfaction, and pornography offers a seemingly easy means of relief. We take a drink and our thirst is momentarily abated. But then, we get "thirsty" again. Each time we want something different, something more until we end up in a place we never thought we would be. The flesh is never satisfied; it always thirsts for more. "*Everyone who drinks this water will thirst again.*"

"Since they no longer have any sense of shame, they have become promiscuous. They practice every kind of sexual perversion <u>with a constant desire for more</u>" (Ephesians 4:19 God's Word Translation).

Like the woman at the well going from one man to another, we go from one porn movie, or one impure relationship to another, acknowledging that once we "drink" of one impure experience, we are soon thirsty for another. Impurity never satisfies. *"Everyone drinks this water will thirst again."* We will have *"a constant desire for more."*

But there is a way to be entirely free from this constant thirsting, and it is to turn from "this water" and learn how to drink "the water Jesus gives." Jesus said, "Everyone who drinks this water will thirst again but *whoever drinks the water I give will never thirst."*

Do you want to have your thirst quenched eternally? Do you want to stop the cycle of thirst/porn/thirst/impurity/thirst/gratify/thirst, etc.? There is a way to be free from it all. Jesus said, *"whoever drinks the water I give will never thirst."*

Turn away from the impure well, turn away from all forms of fleshly gratification, stop drinking at the well of sexual impurity. *"Run from sexual sin! No other sin so clearly affects the body as this one does. For sexual immorality is a sin against your own body"* (1 Corinthians 6:18).

Come to Jesus and learn how to drink from Him. Quench your thirst in Him! Remember Jesus' words, *"whoever drinks the water I give will never thirst!"* Ah, drink up! That's how to be free!

When we come back together, we'll see what happened to this Samaritan woman, and discover what happens when we turn to the water Jesus gives and learn how to quench our thirst in it.

Let's pray, and then we will join our small groups.

Walking By the Spirit
Freedom By the Spirit

Question 1: In Romans 8:1, Paul tells us there is no condemnation for us who are in Christ. In Romans 8:2, what is it that the Spirit of God does for us?

Answer: The Holy Spirit applies the work of Christ on the cross to our hearts and *"sets us free from the law of sin and death."*

Question 2: Would you like to thank God right now that there is no condemnation for you since you have put faith in Jesus Christ? Please write out your thoughts here.

Answer: Allow time for expressions of thankfulness to God.

Question 3: According to Romans 8:3, what did God do for you, and according to Romans 8:4 what should the result be in your life?

Answer: God sent His Son to be our sin offering, and by removing our sin He made a way for the Holy Spirit to live in us, so we can begin to live according to the Spirit, not the flesh.

It would be helpful at this point to connect this answer to the story in John chapter 4 of Jesus meeting with the woman at the well. Read John 7:37-39:

> *John 7:37-39 (NLT) On the last day, the climax of the festival, Jesus stood and shouted to the crowds, "Anyone who is thirsty may come to me! 38 Anyone who believes in me may come and drink! For the Scriptures declare, 'Rivers of living water will flow*

from his heart.'" 39 (When he said "living water," he was speaking of the Spirit, who would be given to everyone believing in him. But the Spirit had not yet been given, because Jesus had not yet entered into his glory.)

Through Jesus' death and resurrection, He removed our sin and thereby made us the temple of the Living God (1 Corinthians 6:20). The Holy Spirit lives in each believer now, and He is the "Living Water" to whom Jesus referred.

To experience the Holy Spirit is to have our thirst quenched. When we walk by the Spirit, we do not gratify the lusts of our flesh (Galatians 5:16).

We must always connect the Spirit of God with the cross of Christ. Just as Moses struck the rock and water flowed out of it to the thirsty Israelites, so Jesus Christ was struck on the cross and out of His death flows the Holy Spirit (1 Corinthians 10:4). So, if we want to drink in the Spirit and quench our thirst eternally, we must go to the cross where the Spirit flows.

Question 4: What does the Spirit of God do for us?
- ☐ He sets us free from slavery.
- ☐ He frees us from fear.
- ☐ He makes us intimate with the Father where we cry "ABBA!"
- ☐ He testifies with our spirit that we are children of God.
- ☐ All of the above.

Answer: All of the above.

Question 5: Please consider your life for just a moment: are the Word of God and the Spirit of God making changes in you? Please share.

Answer: Encourage students to share.

Washing at the Cross
Looking to Christ

Question 1: Please fill in the blanks: "For if you possess these qualities in increasing measure, they will keep you from being _____ and _____ in your knowledge of our Lord Jesus Christ.

Answer: Ineffective; unproductive.

Question 2: According to 2 Peter 1:9, if we are not growing in the qualities of Jesus Christ, what is our problem?
- ☐ We have stopped trying to keep God's Law.
- ☐ We have fallen from grace and are now condemned.
- ☐ We have become nearsighted and blind and have forgotten we were cleansed at the cross.

Answer: We have become nearsighted and blind and have forgotten we were cleansed at the cross.

Question 3: What did the Israelites need to do to be free of the venom from the snakebites?
- ☐ Cut the spot where they were bitten and suck out the poison.
- ☐ Examine the wound, consider its depth and attempt to drain the venom.
- ☐ Look at an uplifted pole with a snake on it.

Answer: Look at an uplifted pole with a snake on it.

It's important to note here that the world would have us fix our attention on the snakebite or the snake. It would want us to study deeply the statistics associated with snakes, the effects of snake venom on the body and brain, and all the scientific aspects of how venom interacts with the human body. For the Israelites to do this would have meant suffering and death by snakebite.

For us to focus on the scientific/medical aspects of what the world calls "addiction" is contrary to God's plan, goes against God's clear command for us to "*fix your eyes on Jesus*" (Hebrews 12:2), and is the opposite of God's wisdom shown at the cross.

> *1 Corinthians 1:25 (NLT) This foolish plan of God is wiser than the wisest of human plans, and God's weakness is stronger than the greatest of human strength.*

Question 4: What does the message to "turn and look" (Numbers 21:8) point forward to, according to Jesus' statement in John 3:15-16?

Answer: The Israelites "turning and looking" at the uplifted pole corresponds to *"everyone who <u>believes</u> may have eternal life"* in John 3:15-16.

Question 5: In Hebrews 12:2, what are we told to focus on?
- ☐ Jesus.
- ☐ Our past woundedness.
- ☐ Our damaged emotions.

Answer: Jesus.

Question 6: In Hebrews 12:2-3, what specifically about Jesus are we to focus on? Please fill in the blank: For the joy set before him he _____ ____ _____, scorning its shame, and sat down at the right hand of the throne of God.

Answer: Endured the cross.

The cross is the believer's solution to the sin problem. It shows Jesus becoming your sin that you might become the righteousness of God (2 Corinthians 5:21). It shows *you* being put to death in the person of Christ (Romans 6:5) so that there is no more penalty for you to pay and the power of sin is broken (Romans 6:7). It shows Jesus assuming *your* guilt, and being condemned in *your* place so that you will be free of guilt and never be condemned (Romans 8:1). This, and so much more, is what we find at the cross.

Question 7: According to Hebrews 12:3 what will the effect be of looking to the cross and considering it?

Answer: We are to turn to Jesus and "fix our eyes on Him," and in so doing, we do not "lose heart." We are strengthened to endure our own death *to* sin as we see Jesus dying *as* sin. We are not only cut down, humbled in our hearts by viewing the cross, but we are also built up, encouraged in heart, strengthened and established by viewing the cross. It does all these things simultaneously.

Question 8: What did you learn, or what have you been reminded of in this lesson?

Answer: Encourage sharing.

LESSON 18:

Washing at the Cross
Seeing Jesus

Question 1: Do you see the importance of seeking freedom by God's chosen method, the cross of Jesus Christ, and not by worldly wisdom? Please share your thoughts.

Answer: The scientific/medical study of brain chemistry, neuron receptors, hormones, etc. does not set captives free. One of the volunteer Setting Captives Free mentors, Mike Nelson, put it this way, "*The feel-good hormones that are released during sex include oxytocin, epinephrine, dopamine, etc. and they were created by God to help us bond to our spouse. When we sin, to what do the chemicals help us bind/attach? Sin and more sin! Doing things God's ways are always best: "For the wisdom of this world is folly with God. For it is written, "He catches the wise in their craftiness," (1 Corinthians 3:19).*

The world considers the message of the cross foolishness and attempts to foist upon believers the need to study the science and psychology of addiction/recovery, but these studies are a distraction and a waste of time. Such things leave us in bondage.

God's method, on the other hand, is to choose something powerless like a cross, something despised like Jesus shedding His blood, to set captives free and thereby bring to nothing all the wisdom of the world.

> *1 Corinthians 1:27-31 (NLT) Instead, God chose things the world considers foolish in order to shame those who think they are wise. And he chose things that are powerless to shame those who are powerful. 28 God chose things despised by the world, things counted as nothing at all, and used them to bring to nothing what*

the world considers important. 29 As a result, no one can ever boast in the presence of God. 30 God has united you with Christ Jesus. For our benefit God made him to be wisdom itself. Christ made us right with God; he made us pure and holy, and he freed us from sin. 31 Therefore, as the Scriptures say, "If you want to boast, boast only about the Lord."

Question 2: What was the solution that God gave Moses to heal the snake-bitten Israelites?

☐ He told Moses to teach about the venom, how it invades the bloodstream and affects the mind of the one bitten.

☐ He told Moses to use the Law to punish all who were rebellious.

☐ He told Moses to lift up a pole with a snake on it, and invite all who were bitten to look and live.

Answer: He told Moses to lift up a pole with a snake on it, and invite all who were bitten to look and live.

Question 3: What do you see when looking at the cross of Christ?

Answer: We want participants to examine the cross, to see the glory and beauty of it, the power and love of God in it. This causes us to give up our sin and turn from all our pride.

Question 4: What are your thoughts about the wrath of God being entirely spent on Jesus so that none of it is left for you?

Answer: Help participants to understand that Jesus drank the full cup of God's wrath for them (Jeremiah 25:15; Mark 10:38), took all the arrows of God's hatred of sin for them, and saved them completely from God's wrath (1 Thessalonians 1:10).

Question 5: Please explain what it feels like to see Jesus taking your sins on Himself and removing them far from you forever.

Answer: Let all share, time permitting.

Washing at the Cross

Fix Your Eyes on Jesus

Question 1: What more do you see as you look at the cross today?

Answer: All can share.

Question 2: Please fill in the blank: I am not a captive of sin and death, I have been set free because Jesus gave Himself as my _____. The price He paid is His own _____.

Answer: Ransom; blood.

Question 3: True or false: Jesus Christ entered the darkness and died on the cross to rescue me from the power of darkness, and I am now free!

Answer: True!

Question 4: Cursed is everyone who is _____ _____ __ _____ . Jesus was cursed that I might be _____ with the Holy Spirit.

Answer: Hung on a pole; blessed.

Question 5: What does it mean to you, personally, that Jesus went to a cross to redeem you from an empty life and fill you with His Spirit? Please share your thoughts:

Answer: Unique to the student.

Question 6: How have you been reconciled to God and made His friend?
- ☐ By your efforts to do better and quit sinning.
- ☐ By the cross of Jesus Christ.
- ☐ By becoming obedient to the Law of God and following His commandments.

Answer: By the cross of Jesus Christ.

God chose a cross to reconcile His people. Jesus' death is the great magnet that draws all people to Jesus (John 12:32) and makes enemies into friends (Ephesians 2:14).

The devil blinds unbelievers to this glorious reality of a crucified Christ (2 Corinthians 4:4). He tells us we can work off our sin debt and keep our pride. He wants us to be religious and take steps to our freedom so that we might boast of how many days free we are or how long we've been in recovery. This is foolishness, whereas the cross is true wisdom (1 Corinthians 1:27-31).

Question 7: What have you learned in this lesson and how will it set you free?

Answer: Allow for haring.

Warring Against Our Flesh
Through Prayer

Question 1: How is your battle plan going? Does it need adjusting, or is it bearing the fruit of freedom in your life?

Answer: Help people to understand the need to change their strategy if it is not working adequately, to adjust their plan so that there are no areas where Satan can slip through the cracks. It is crucial that we shore up our defenses and change tactics as needed, so that "having done all...to stand" (Galatians 6:13).

Question 2: Have you been praying earnestly for Jesus to set you free? Please share your thoughts.

Answer: Unique to the student.

Question 3: What can we learn about prayer from considering Jacob's night of wrestling with God?
- ☐ The Double-Nelson hold works best when wrestling with God.
- ☐ It takes boldness and perseverance, tenacity and a refusal to let God go until He blesses us with freedom.
- ☐ God can be overcome in a wrestling match.

Answer: It takes boldness and perseverance, tenacity and a refusal to let God go until He blesses us with freedom.

Question 4: Please fill in the blank. "I tell you, even though he will not get up and give him anything just because he is his friend, yet because of his _____ and _____ he will get up and give him whatever he needs."

Answer: Persistence; boldness.

Question 5: What do you learn from this Canaanite woman's encounter with Jesus?

Answer: She would not take no for an answer. She pressed through many barriers to get what she needed but did so humbly.

Question 6: What does God promise us when we go to His throne of grace?
- ☐ Rebuke and chastisement for our life of sin.
- ☐ Anger and lashings for our disobedience.
- ☐ Mercy and grace.

Answer: Mercy and grace. Jesus' death on the cross should provide strong assurance for all to come to the throne of grace, for Jesus' blood has opened the way.

Moses was required to build a barrier around the mountain where God gave the Law, and God instructed Moses to tell all people to keep out and stay away, or they would be put to death (Exodus 19:10-13). His holiness cannot bear the presence of sin. The law keeps us away from God.

In the gospel, the fence was torn down, the curtain of the temple was torn from top to bottom, Jesus' blood opened the way, and all are invited to come near.

Question 7: What did you learn from this lesson today?

Answer: Allow time for sharing.

Summary teaching by the leader: 10 minutes

Welcome back to our final teaching session for this week. Let's get started.

During the discussion time, did you notice that Jesus explained what "Living Water" is? Jesus announced:

> *John 7:37-39 (NIV) On the last and greatest day of the festival, Jesus stood and said in a loud voice, "Let anyone who is thirsty come to me and drink. 38 Whoever believes in me, as Scripture has said, rivers of living water will flow from within them." 39 By this, he meant the Spirit, whom those who believed in him were later to receive.*

This is a vital understanding. The Holy Spirit alone quenches our thirst. A man can have the entire Bible memorized and still thirst, crave, lust and yearn because he hasn't come to the cross to receive the Spirit. A person might be religious, doing many good things, giving themselves in service or ministering to orphans and widows and making an impact in the culture, yet be unsatisfied and longing for more. This is because they have not seen and embraced the cross of Jesus and received the Holy Spirit.

With that in mind, let's return to John 4 and the account of the conversation between Jesus and the Samaritan woman by Jacob's well. We remember that Jesus said, "Everyone who drinks this water will thirst again, but whoever drinks the water I give will never thirst."

At this point, the Samaritan woman tries to divert the conversation, as many of us would when confronted with our sin, and she asks about where she should worship. Jesus replies that real worship is not at a place but in a person. When someone comes to Jesus and drinks His living water, the Spirit of God produces worship in their hearts.

When it's a hot day outside, and you receive a drink of cool, refreshing water and respond with, "Ahhh!" in satisfaction; that's like worship. When we believe in Jesus, that He removed our sin from us, made us right with God, paid our penalty for sin, and gave us eternal life, and respond with overflowing gratitude; that's worship.

Through further conversation, Jesus revealed Himself as the Messiah to this Samaritan woman; she believed Him and ran to tell the whole town about Jesus. In her hurry to tell others, this woman does something significant:

> *John 4:28-30 (NIV) Then, leaving her water jar, the woman went back to the town and said to the people, 29 "Come, see a man who told me everything I ever did. Could this be the Messiah?" 30 They came out of the town and made their way toward him.*

She had made such a discovery and had her deepest thirst quenched in Jesus that she abandoned her original purpose for coming to the well. She left her water jar behind in her eagerness to tell others.

Friend, do you want to know what will enable you to leave behind impurity? It's learning to drink of Jesus Christ. Believing in His death and resurrection, and receiving the Holy Spirit, who is Living Water. The Spirit gives us such joy in Jesus, such thankfulness for His cross, such satisfaction in our hearts that we, too, can leave behind "this water."

In closing, let us not miss the foreshadowing of the gospel itself in this story. Think of it: the disciples left Jesus hungry as they went into town to get food (John 4:8), and the woman at the well left Him thirsty, as she never provided Him a drink of water. And yet, in the midst of His hunger and thirst, Jesus gave living water and eternal life to one who needed it. He thirsted, she was quenched.

When Jesus was on the cross, He said, "I thirst!" (John 19:28). And it was profoundly true: Jesus had fully entered into the human condition of thirsting and had taken on our sin to the point of becoming sin which is always associated with thirsting, craving, and yearning. And while Jesus hung there on the cross in the agony of pain and thirst, He worked to quench your thirst and satisfy your soul. He poured out His life and His Spirit for you so that you might have your thirst assuaged forever! He thirsted, you are quenched. Do you understand? Have you grasped this beautiful truth?

Let's pray.

Suggested Songs
Come Thou Fount of Every Blessing
Holy Spirit Living Breath of God by Keith and Kristyn Getty
Behold (Then Sings My Soul) by Hillsong Worship

Week 5

- **Welcome of all students, leader prayer for the meeting: 5 minutes**
- **Introductory teaching by the leader: 10 minutes**

*W*elcome back; it is good to see you continuing in the study!

As we start our session, we are going to look at two characteristics of Jesus Christ, and then see how they relate to our desire for purity. We'll look at the first one here in this session, then the second one before we leave.

Let's look at Isaiah chapter 50. Chapter 50 begins a section of the book of Isaiah that focuses on God's suffering and obedient servant, which we know is a reference to Jesus Christ. Jesus is speaking through the prophet Isaiah and let's read what He says starting in verse 6. Isaiah 50 verse 6 and 7:

> *"I offered my back to those who beat me and my cheeks to those who pulled out my beard. I did not hide my face from mockery and spitting. 7 Because the Sovereign Lord helps me, I will not be disgraced. Therefore, I have set my face like a stone, determined to do his will. And I know that I will not be put to shame." Isaiah 50:6-7 (NLT)*

Here was a man, whom we know to be the God-man Jesus Christ who was determined to do God's will. He "set His face like a stone," showing His courage and firm commitment to accomplish what God had sent Him to do; and this in spite of all the scorn and hatred heaped upon Him. The Messiah was dedicated to one thing in life: He came to do the will of the Father.

When we come to the New Testament, we read in Luke 9:51 *"As the time drew near for him to ascend to heaven, Jesus resolutely set out for Jerusalem."* This is the New Testament fulfillment of Isaiah 50. Jesus was firmly determined to go to Jerusalem where He would have His beard pulled out, where He would purposefully offer His back to be beaten and His face to be spit upon and where

He would be crucified. Spend just a moment considering how much Jesus loves you, to endure mocking, spitting, beating, piercing and death for you.

Jesus' firm resolve is what we want to emulate. He "set His face like a stone," meaning He would not look left or right, would not be distracted or dissuaded from going to the cross, no matter the cost to Himself personally.

We need this supernatural resolve to press on and persevere in purity. We're at week five now, and we can all acknowledge that dying to our fleshly desires is hard! It requires us to set our face like flint. It requires courage and determination.

Jesus was determined to go to the cross. He was dead set on fulfilling the salvation plan that He, the Father, and the Spirit developed in eternity past. His face was set, His mind resolute, and His heart filled with sacrificial love. To the cross, He was determined to go, and to the cross, He went!

Friends, let's consider Jesus' determination and be empowered by it. This change in our lifestyle of washing at the cross, walking by the Spirit and warring against our flesh is not a temporary one. We need to be resolved to live this way for the rest of our lives. Let us be flint-faced about it, determined to do the will of the Father no matter the suffering, keeping our eyes on Jesus all through life. Let's pray.

Warring Against our Flesh
Praying God's Word

Question 1: What are the two requirements to receiving whatever we ask for in prayer?

- ☐ That we are obedient to the Law and that we walk by the Spirit.
- ☐ That we remain in Christ, and His words remain in us.
- ☐ That we overcome sin and bear fruit to God's glory.

Answer: That we remain in Christ and His words remain in us.

Question 2: Please write out your prayer to God using His actual words from Psalm 107:10-16:

Answer: This is usually a precious time for the student to pray God's Word back to Him, and to share that prayer with the class.

Question 3: This is your place to pray God's Word back to Him, believing He will honor His Word and hear your prayer.

Answer: Help students understand that it's not just personalizing God's Word; it's actually putting faith in God's Word that makes the difference and believing it to be true for them. Embracing the cross as personal to them and considering it to be true for them.

Question 4: What did you learn in this lesson today and how will you apply it in your life?

Answer: Let all students share, time permitting.

Warring Against the Flesh
Practical Battle Plans

Question 1: Have you humbled yourself to ask for help from a pastor, elder, teacher, Christian friend or family member? Please share.

Answer: In essence, that is what we are all doing together here, expressing our need for each other, asking for help and humbling ourselves to listen to God's Word and to pray for each other.

Question 2: Please fill in the blank: you who live by the Spirit should _____ that person gently.

Answer: Restore.

Question 3: Please write out Proverbs 15:32 NIV. As you are writing, take time to think about the verse.

Answer: The humble listen to counsel from God's Word, the prideful ignore it and continue on the road to ruin.

Question 4: According to Ecclesiastes 4:9 NIV, why are two better than one?
- ☐ They can make more money working together.
- ☐ Each person's strengths combine to make both stronger.
- ☐ They have a good return for their labor.

Answer: They have a good return for their labor.

Question 5: What is the subject of Ecclesiastes 4:10?
- ☐ Restoration - helping the fallen one up.
- ☐ Salvation - saving from God's wrath.
- ☐ Intercession - praying for others.

Answer: Restoration - helping the fallen one up.

Question 6: According to Ecclesiastes 4:11, what is the value of two walking together?
- ☐ They hold each other up.
- ☐ They keep warm together.
- ☐ They protect each other.

Answer: They keep warm together. We're talking in this passage about the spiritual value of "one another," to help each other keep warm. One of the greatest ways to do that is to share with others where God is showing you the gospel of Jesus Christ in the Bible. Share with one another your findings, how God is opening your eyes to see Jesus in His Word. This is how we "keep warm together."

Question 7: How does Ecclesiastes 4:12 figure into our strategy of warring against our flesh?

Answer: It's easy to be overpowered by the evil one when you're alone, so wise people take precaution when going into situations of being alone. The author of this course, Mike Cleveland, has learned to Skype often with his wife Jody when they have to be apart. He also uses an app called "Marco Polo" to send encouraging messages to his wife, family, friends, and the board members of Setting Captives Free. Using these means, he can pray, share and worship with lots of family and friends no matter where they are.

Question 8: What is the value of asking for help in our fight against impurity?

Answer: The main value is in the humility that comes when we lower ourselves and explain our problems and ask for help with them. This can set us on a course of humbling ourselves before the Lord and seeking His help and guidance.

Warring Against the Flesh
Abiding in Christ

Question 1: According to Romans 12:2, how are we transformed?
- ☐ By renewing our minds.
- ☐ By rejecting the world's lies and embracing God's truth.
- ☐ By remaining (abiding) in Christ.
- ☐ All of the above.

Answer: All of the above.

Question 2: Why is it important to not be conformed to the world's mold but rather be transformed by renewing our minds in the truth of God's Word? Please share your thoughts.

Answer: The world's mold will always end in us following the god of this world and being enslaved to our flesh (Ephesians 2:1-3). We must reject the world's labels and words and its intention to keep us in bondage, and turn to God's Word and be transformed by the renewing of our minds (Romans 12:2).

This renewing of our minds in Scripture always happens with the cross in full view, even as the passage telling us to be transformed by renewing our minds starts with the words, "In view of God's mercy…" (Romans 12:1). We see God's mercy, in the Jew's rejection of the Messiah so that you might receive grace and acceptance, in Jesus' sufferings on Calvary for you so that you might be free, in Jesus' shedding His last drop of blood and breathing out the Holy Spirit for you so that you might be given life and filled, etc. In view of all God's mercy, "be transformed by renewing your mind."

Question 3: What are you called in John 15:1-2 NCV?
- ☐ The Vine.
- ☐ The Gardener.
- ☐ A branch.

Answer: A branch.

Question 4: What does the Father do for you if you start to bear fruit? Fill in the blank: And he trims and _____ every branch that produces fruit so that it will produce even more fruit.

Answer: Cleans.

Question 5: According to John 15, what effect does the Word of God have on all who believe it?
- ☐ It convicts us of sin.
- ☐ It makes us sinless.
- ☐ It cleanses our hearts and minds.

Answer: It cleanses our hearts and minds.

Question 6: According to John 15:4, how can you produce fruit, escape the trap of habitual sin, and be free from lust? Please share your thoughts.

Answer: Only by remaining in Christ, living in His love, dwelling at the foot of the cross and receiving fresh mercy and new grace every day.

Question 7: According to John 15:7, how do we remain in Christ?
- ☐ Bible study and prayer.
- ☐ Stop sinning.
- ☐ Be baptized at a church.

Answer: Bible study and prayer. Remaining in Christ is not limited to Bible study and prayer; we also remain in Christ when we do not gratify the lusts of our flesh, when we go to church and hear gospel-centered sermons, when we worship and give and serve others in love, etc.

Question 8: According to Exodus 28:38 NIV, what would Aaron, the High priest, bear, and what would be the result? "...he will bear the _____ involved in the sacred gifts the Israelites consecrate, whatever their gifts may be. It will be on Aaron's forehead continually so that _____ _____ ____ _____ to the Lord.

Answer: Guilt; They will be acceptable. And here is the gospel. Jesus, our High Priest, bore our guilt on His forehead as a crown of thorns, to make us acceptable to the Father.

Question 9: What did you receive from this lesson today, and how will you apply it?

Answer: Let all answer, time permitting.

Warring Against the Flesh
Believing God's Word

Question 1: According to Hebrews 4:2 NCV, why did the good news of the gospel not help the Israelites who heard it?

Answer: They did not combine it with faith. They did not believe the gospel applied to them, personally. They did not internalize it, so they did not receive any benefit from it. We must hear and believe the gospel, ourselves. We must derive benefit from it by putting faith in it. We must apply it to our lives.

Question 2: According to John 5:46-47 NCV, what was the main problem with how the Pharisees read the Old Testament?
- ☐ The read it in a hurry and didn't stop to meditate on it.
- ☐ They didn't see Jesus in it and didn't believe the gospel.
- ☐ They read it to tell others what to do, not for their benefit.

Answer: They didn't see Jesus in it and didn't believe the gospel.

Here is the danger of reading God's Word out of context, or reading the written Word but not seeing the Living Word in it. To miss Jesus in the Word is to read into Scripture something that is not meant by it. That is called "Eisegesis" where we read into God's Word some message other than what God was communicating.

We only exegete or pull out of God's Word rightly, when we keep the Living Word and the written Word together; that is, when we see Jesus and His finished work throughout the pages of Scripture.

Question 3: Why do you need to both hear the gospel and accept it with faith?

Answer: We need to hear it ongoingly and believe it continually, for *"whatever is not from faith is sin"* (Romans 14:23). We could stop viewing porn, break off adulterous relationships, free ourselves from Bible-condemned but culture-approved lifestyles, but still be in sin if we are not doing these things by faith in the gospel for the glory of God.

　When we read/hear the gospel of Jesus Christ and believe it, the Holy Spirit becomes active in our lives and leads us away from impurity. This is the gospel-centric, Holy Spirit-empowered way to be free.

Question 4: What two concepts do we see combined in Romans 10:11-13?
- ☐ Believing and calling on the Lord.
- ☐ Reading Scripture and experiencing God's blessing.
- ☐ Jews and Gentiles finding salvation.

Answer: Believing and calling on the Lord.

Question 5: Please consider how Isaiah 53:5 applies to you and then write it out in a personal manner. Make it specific to you and your situation.

Answer: We do not want students to merely substitute the word "our" for the word "my" here, but to think through how this passage applies personally to them and to write it out in that way. Encourage sharing.

Question 6: Please write out Isaiah 53:10 in a believing way:

Answer: Same as Question 5.

Question 7: What did you learn today and how will you apply it?

Answer: Let all share, time permitting.

Warring Against the Flesh
Overcoming Bitterness

Question 1: How are things going now? Are you walking by the Spirit or in the flesh? Is there anything about your plan that needs to change? If so, what will you change?

Answer: Do not accept excuses or ignore comments such as, "My situation is so unique, I just can't get free." That is faithless talk, that is fearful talk, that is selfish talk, and that is ungodly talk. If you see the cross and believe it, not only will you get free, you will be free *indeed* (John 8:32)!

If anyone is still falling into sexual sin, ask them in what way they are falling, and then give all participants a chance to share how the one falling could make changes to overcome. Usually, and especially in large groups, many people will have wise counsel to share that will help the one still stumbling.

This is carrying the weaker brother or sister, and helping them to "catch up." When the Israelites were leaving Egypt the frail, elderly and lame would lag behind and get picked off by enemy armies. The role of the church is to help the laggards and the lame to catch up and walk in safety with the rest of the body.

> *Isaiah 35:3-4 (NIV) Strengthen the feeble hands, steady the knees that give way; 4 say to those with fearful hearts, "Be strong, do not fear; your God will come, he will come with vengeance; with divine retribution, he will come to save you."*

> *Hebrews 12:12-13 (NIV) Therefore, strengthen your feeble arms and weak knees. 13 "Make level paths for your feet," so that the lame may not be disabled, but rather healed.*

Question 2: According to Hebrews 12:15, what does bitterness do in our lives?
- ☐ Causes trouble and defiles many people.
- ☐ Makes our hearts full of noxious compounds like carbon dioxide.
- ☐ Nothing, it's undetectable in our hearts.

Answer: Causes trouble and defiles many people.

Question 3: Why could the Israelites not drink the water?
- ☐ It was bitter.
- ☐ It was frozen.
- ☐ It was salty.

Answer: It was bitter.

Question 4: What was the solution for the bitter water? "Then Moses cried out to the Lord, and the Lord showed him a _____ ____ _____ " (Exodus 15:25 NIV).

Answer: Piece of wood.

Question 5: What does 1 Peter 2:24 call the place where Jesus bore our sins and healed us?
- ☐ A cave
- ☐ A tree
- ☐ A rock

Answer: A tree.

Question 6: According to Galatians 3:13, where did Jesus redeem you from the curse of the Law?
- ☐ On a rock.
- ☐ On a tree.
- ☐ In heaven.

Answer: On a tree.

Question 7: Do you now see the way to be made pure and overcome the bitterness that comes from impurity? Please explain:

Answer: Bitterness in the heart keeps us in bondage to sin. All bitterness is extracted from the heart at the cross, and removed from our lives through the application of the gospel and the work of the Spirit.

Question 8: Do you relate to Matthew's testimony? Please share your thoughts.

Answer: Answers will vary.

Summary teaching by the leader: 10 minutes

Welcome back, hope you had a great discussion time today.

During our opening talk today, we saw Jesus' steadfast determination to go to Jerusalem where He would suffer in our place and die our death. He was committed to the will of the Father clear to the very end, clear unto death.

As followers of Jesus, we need that kind of resolution to follow through clear to the end.

As we close out today, I wanted to look with you not only at Jesus' resolve but also at His perseverance. It's one thing to resolve to do something; it's quite another to persevere clear to the end. To live to the glory of God and not to the craving of our flesh, and to do so for the rest of our lives requires not only resolve but also perseverance.

Let's notice for just a moment the perseverance of Jesus:

When He was betrayed by Judas and abandoned by all His disciples, He kept going. When He was falsely accused, He persevered. When He was flogged, He kept going, when He was beaten He didn't stop, when He was mocked and spit on, He stayed the course.

And when God laid the sins of the world on Him - all impurity, lying, disobedience of all kinds, right on Him - He kept going! When the Father laid all sicknesses on Him - cancer, HIV, Parkinson's, heart disease, and diabetes - right on His Son - Jesus didn't stop. God made Jesus, the spotless Lamb of God, an offering for sin - the righteous for the unrighteous, the holy and pure for the unholy and impure - and Jesus kept going, kept persevering!

Finally, Jesus was taken to the top of the hill called Calvary, the Place of the Skull; would He then shrink back and call for a legion of angels to deliver Him? No, He pressed on! He laid down on that wood and received the nails pounded into His flesh, **one, two, three**, and the spear into His side. You can practically hear Jesus saying "Keep going, keep pounding, keep stabbing, I have to reach the end, I have to save you and set you free!" And He did die, and they buried him.

But even the grave could not stop Him. The grave couldn't keep Him in, and the walls where the disciples were meeting couldn't keep Him out - He had to get to His disciples, He had to show them the wounds in His hands and feet and side, and reveal to them that they now had forgiveness of sins and peace with God through His wounds.

He persevered beyond the grave, and even Mary, clinging to Him as you and I would, didn't stop Him. "Let me go; I have to get to my Father." And so He went right back to heaven.

And finally, even the gates in heaven couldn't keep the conquering King out!

Open up, ancient gates!
Open up, ancient doors,
and let the King of glory enter.
8 Who is the King of glory?
The Lord, strong and mighty;
the Lord, invincible in battle.
9 Open up, ancient gates!
Open up, ancient doors,
and let the King of glory enter.
10 Who is the King of glory?
The Lord of Heaven's Armies—
he is the King of glory.
Psalms 24:7-10 (NLT)

This is our Suffering and Conquering King! And this is our persevering Example!

2 Thessalonians 3:5 (NIV) May the Lord direct your hearts into
God's love and Christ's perseverance.

Closing prayer

Suggested Songs
Jesus Paid it All (All to Him I Owe)
Death was Arrested by North Point InsideOut
It is Finished by Matt Redman

Week 6

- **Welcome of all students, leader prayer for the meeting: 5 minutes**
- **Introductory teaching by the leader: 10 minutes**

*W*elcome back; you've made it to the final week of this study! This week I'm excited to share with you about what it means to have victory in Jesus. Now, we all know that we are in a battle: the flesh wars against the spirit, and the spirit wars against the flesh. Our flesh craves gratification, but the Holy Spirit leads us away from a lifestyle of self-indulgence and into the victorious life of crucifixion and resurrection.

Let's take a moment now to look at a couple of passages that show us our victory is in Jesus, and in our closing session, I will show you an illustration of this very thing. Our first text is:

> *Deuteronomy 20:1-4 (NIV) When you go to war against your enemies and see horses and chariots and an army greater than yours, do not be afraid of them, because the Lord your God, who brought you up out of Egypt, will be with you. 2 When you are about to go into battle, the priest shall come forward and address the army. 3 He shall say: "Hear, Israel: Today you are going into battle against your enemies. Do not be fainthearted or afraid; do not panic or be terrified by them. 4 For the Lord your God is the one who goes with you to fight for you against your enemies to give you victory."*

When the Israelites faced armies greater than themselves they were told not to fear them. Did you notice why? *"because the Lord your God, who brought you up out of Egypt, will be with you"* (Deuteronomy 20:1).

Three times God said similar words: "do not be afraid...do not fainthearted or afraid...do not panic or be terrified," and each time the reason was given, "*For the Lord your God is the One who goes with you to fight for you against your enemies to give you victory!*" (Deuteronomy 20:4).

This is true for us as well. We have nothing to fear when it comes to fighting for our freedom from impurity, for our God is with us, and He is fighting for us to give us the victory. The God who came down to the cross to bring us up out of slavery is the same God who fights with us and for us today.

The New Testament states it plainly, "*The sting of death is sin, and the power of sin is the law. But thanks be to God! He gives us the victory through our Lord Jesus Christ*" (1 Corinthians 15:56-57). Here God promises us victory over sin and death, through Jesus Christ our Lord. Jesus died on the cross and won our victory over sin, and He rose from the dead and won our victory over death. We win!

So, in the battle against our flesh, the evil one, and the allurements of the world, we have the promise of victory sealed in blood and made real by resurrection power.

There is no need to fear the desires of our flesh, the enticements of the porn industry, or the wiles of Satan. Jesus has given up His life willingly, has risen from the dead victorious guaranteeing our victory over the world, our flesh, and the devil. So, do not fear, instead, look to Jesus crucified and risen in power, making you more than a conqueror through Him Who loved you.

His victory means that we win the battle over our flesh. Looking at Jesus' suffering for us and His glories which followed gives us spiritual power to reject all porn, turning away from all sexual impurity.

Yes, our God is more powerful than our flesh. Our weak heart becomes strong in Christ. Our God is stronger than Satan and the evil powers of this world, and He is for us. And when He promises victory in Christ, victory is ours! We win! Let's pray.

Warring Against the Flesh
God's Provision in Marriage

Question 1: When Paul writes in Ephesians 5:31-32 about man and wife being united together, becoming one flesh, about whom is he talking?
- ☐ Himself and his wife.
- ☐ Believers and their spouses.
- ☐ Christ and the church.

Answer: Christ and the church.

Question 2: According to 1 Corinthians 7:1-2 NIV, what is God's provision for those struggling with sexual immorality? Fill in the blank: "But since sexual immorality is occurring, each man should have sexual relations with his _____ wife, and each woman with her _____ husband.

Answer: Own; own.

Question 3: According to 1 Corinthians 7:5 NIV, why are spouses not to deprive each other sexually?

☐ So that Satan will not tempt you because of your lack of self-control.

☐ So that you can have children together.

☐ So that you can express love for each other often.

Answer: So that Satan will not tempt you because of your lack of self-control. This is important. A husband and wife are exhorted in this chapter to make sure they do not stay apart sexually, except for a time and by mutual consent, *"so that Satan will not tempt you because of your lack of self-control"* (1 Corinthians 7:5).

A few years ago, the "90-day sex fast" became very popular in therapy circles. The idea was that abstaining from sex for three months would help the one in bondage to impurity.

But abstinence from sex within marriage, though having an appearance of wisdom, is not God's method of freeing one from slavery to impurity. Just the opposite, we are told to not withhold from each other, but rather to come together within marriage to be a united front against the evil one and his temptations.

Here is a passage to consider reading to the group, if any believe the worldly argument of abstaining over the truth of God's Word:

> *Colossians 2:20-23 (NIV) Since you died with Christ to the elemental spiritual forces of this world, why, as though you still belonged to the world, do you submit to its rules: 21 "Do not handle! Do not taste! Do not touch!"? 22 These rules, which have to do with things that are all destined to perish with use, are based on merely human commands and teachings. 23 Such regulations indeed have an appearance of wisdom, with their self-imposed worship, their false humility and their harsh treatment of the body, but they lack any value in restraining sensual indulgence.*

Question 4: According to 1 Corinthians 7:8-9, what are people who are unmarried to do if they have strong sexual desire and find they cannot control themselves?

- ☐ Engage in self-sex.
- ☐ Use a sexual outlet based upon our desires.
- ☐ Marry.

Answer: Marry.

Question 5: Why is marriage God's provision for "burning" with strong desire?

Answer: God gave marriage 1) to be a picture of Christ and His bride, and the intimacy we share together, 2) to be pleasurable for both spouses within marriage, and 3) to propagate the human race.

Question 6: Why is it important to reject all false intimacy experiences and only make use of God' provision for sexuality?

Answer: Anything outside of God's chosen use of sexuality is impurity, brings guilt and shame and leaves us in bondage to the flesh.

Question 7: What did you learn today and how will you apply it?

Answer: Allow time for students to share.

Do not argue with students on this issue. We do not need to defend God's Word. It says what it says, and what it says is clear. If people wish to argue, they need to know they are arguing against God's Word and against their own freedom, they are not arguing with us.

LESSON 27:

Washing at the Cross
Clothed in Christ

Question 1: What are the three foundational principles of freedom?
- ☐ Washing at the cross, walking by the Spirit, warring against the flesh.
- ☐ Promising to be pure, vowing to overcome, meeting with others.
- ☐ Trusting God, trying hard, treasuring Christ.

Answer: Washing at the cross, walking by the Spirit, warring against the flesh.

Question 2: What things do you see, from Genesis 3:6-7, that led to the fall of Adam and Eve?

Answer: They saw beauty in the fruit, thought it would give them wisdom and wanted to be like God.

Question 3: What did Adam and Eve do once they realized they were naked?
- ☐ Repented immediately and came to God for forgiveness.
- ☐ Hid from God and tried to cover their nakedness themselves.
- ☐ Promised never to do that again, and agreed to hold themselves accountable.

Answer: Hid from God and tried to cover their nakedness themselves.

Question 4: What word did Adam use, showing his self-centeredness? ___ heard you in the garden, and _____ was afraid because _____ was naked; so _____ hid."

Answer: I; I; I; I.

Question 5: Adam blamed Eve, but who did he ultimately blame for his sin?

☐ Satan
☐ Himself
☐ God

Answer: God.

Question 6: Why is denying sin or blame-shifting counterproductive to finding freedom?

Answer: As long as we can make our sin someone else's fault then we can avoid repentance and remain in our pride, both of which leave us enslaved. Blame-shifting is part of our fallen nature and spiritual immaturity. When God brings us to our senses, we take responsibility for our sin, humble ourselves and repent, and then grace is poured out, abundant and free, on us from God.

Question 7: What did God do for His children who had sinned, who were naked and exposed, who were under the death sentence?

☐ He executed judgment in wrath and killed them both.
☐ He put them on probation and said He would watch them to see how they did in the future.
☐ He lovingly clothed them with garments of skin.

Answer: He lovingly clothed them with garments of skin.

Question 8: Please take a moment and list what you can learn from God putting to death a substitute in place of Adam and Eve:

Answer: God gave grace where they expected punishment. God forgave them and clothed them out of love. God taught them that they could not clothe themselves by their own efforts; instead, they had to accept God's free gift to be in right standing with Him.

Question 9: What thoughts do you have about the sacrifice of Jesus Christ for you right now?

Answer: Let people share praise to Jesus Christ, the Lamb of God who takes away the sin of the world (John 1:29).

Walking by the Spirit
Brought to Jesus

Question 1: What is the Holy Spirit called and what does He do?
- ☐ Advocate who teaches us all things reminds us of Jesus' words.
- ☐ Sent by the Father in Jesus' name to live in us and walk with us.
- ☐ Comforter who walks with us and enables us to not gratify the lusts of our flesh.
- ☐ All of the above.

Answer: All of the above.

Question 2: What is the role of the Holy Spirit, according to John 15:26?

Answer: He is our Advocate who tells us all about Jesus, drawing us to the Son.

Question 3: Is the Holy Spirit making Jesus precious to you in your life today? Please share:

Answer: Viewing the cross/resurrection of Jesus is what makes Christ precious to all who believe. If He is not precious to some, they need to spend time at Calvary, surveying the wondrous cross.

Question 4: Please fill in the blank. When speaking about the son, the servant says that Abraham "has given him _____ he owns."

Answer: Everything.

Question 5: Please share any thoughts you might have about this lesson today:

Answer: Students should have seen the work of the Holy Spirit illustrated by the story in Genesis 24, and come to appreciate how the Spirit comes to get them and walk them away from their past life, taking them into intimacy with the Son, Jesus Christ.

LESSON 29:

Warring Against the Flesh
Receiving a Battle Plan

Question 1: Do you see that Jesus won the battle over sin and Satan through His death on the cross and that through your death you win too?
- ☐ Yes, Jesus died for sin, and I'm dying to sin, and we are winning!
- ☐ Somewhat, I see victory is through death, and I'm learning how to die to win the battle.
- ☐ No, I'm not dying to sin and am still living in it.

Answer: Allow students the opportunity to share.

Question 2: Are you experiencing resurrection power and Holy Spirit power as you focus on the cross?
- ☐ Yes, most definitely.
- ☐ I'm learning to more and more.
- ☐ No, I've been fighting in my own strength and losing.

Answer: Encourage students to share; rejoice with those who are seeing victory, pray for those who are yet in bondage.

Question 3: David struck down the Philistines and won the battle. How did He win?

☐ He knew he was stronger and could take them easily, so he went out to fight!

☐ He gathered together professional armies to help him win the battle.

☐ He inquired of the Lord and received a specific battle plan to use in the fight.

Answer: He inquired of the Lord and received a specific battle plan to use in the fight.

Question 4: Is your battle plan specific and therefore bringing freedom? Please share.

Answer: Let all share, and if some are not finding success in battle, ask others in the group who are walking in freedom to offer encouragement and gospel-centered counsel on how they would fight the fight in the circumstances of the one falling.

Question 5: Please fill in the blank: "As soon as you hear the sound of marching in the tops of the poplar trees, move quickly, because that will mean _____ _____ ____ _____ ____ ___ _____ of you to strike the Philistine army." (2 Samuel 5:24 NIV)

Answer: the Lord has gone out in front...

Question 6: Why is it important to fight from a position of knowing that God is for you and that the victory is assured?

Answer: We fight confidently, knowing Christ has secured our victory at the cross. We fight deliberately, and we fight triumphantly.

Question 7: What were you reminded of in this lesson and how will you implement it in your life?

Answer: God gives us the victory through our Lord Jesus Christ!

Testimony and Review

Question 1: What are the three foundational principles of freedom?

Answer: Washing at the cross, walking by the Spirit, warring against our flesh.

Question 2: Do you find these principles helpful for you in your walk with Christ?

Answer: Answers will vary, but the hope is that the principles are helpful.

Question 3: What changes have taken place in your life over the previous 30 lessons?

Answer: Let everyone share, if time permits.

Please send any feedback to helpdesk@settingcaptivesfree.com.

Summary teaching by the leader: 10 minutes

I hope you had a great discussion today. Thank you for staying the course and attending our sessions together.

We'll close with a short illustration of the victory that all believers have in Jesus.

God's people, Israel, were once attacked by a powerful army called the Amalekites. We read about their battle in Exodus 17. The leader of God's people, Moses, stated that he and two others would go to the top of a nearby hill and intercede for the army general, Joshua, and pray for their victory.

Let's read the outcome:

> *Exodus 17:10-13 (NIV) So Joshua fought the Amalekites as Moses had ordered, and Moses, Aaron, and Hur went to the top of the hill. 11 As long as Moses held up his hands, the Israelites were winning, but whenever he lowered his hands, the Amalekites were winning. 12 When Moses' hands grew tired, they took a stone and put it under him, and he sat on it. Aaron and Hur held his hands up—one on one side, one on the other—so that his hands remained steady till sunset. 13 So Joshua overcame the Amalekite army with the sword.*

So, in this story, we see three men on a hill, and the one in the middle, Moses, is raising his hands in the picture of intercession and victory. And what we want to be very clear about is what Moses was doing and what result that produced.

Moses is with two other men on a hill, and he has gone up to intercede with God on behalf of the Israelites. *And God made the outcome of this battle totally dependent on what that man in the middle did while he was on the hill.* If his hands were lifted the Israelites won, and if they dropped the Israelites lost. Let me say this again, listen carefully: "*God made the outcome of this battle totally dependent on what that man in the middle did while he was on the hill.*"

Oh, friends, this story is designed to point us to the work of Jesus Christ on the cross. We are attacked on all sides by a great army led by Satan. Even own flesh works against us with its lusts and cravings. Their goal is our defeat and destruction.

But two thousand years ago, God sent His Son up a hill to die on a cross. Jesus was put between two criminals, being *"numbered with the transgressors"* (Isaiah 53:12). His hands were lifted up and nailed to the cross, and God made the outcome of our battle *totally dependent on what that man in the middle did while He was on the hill.* Our victory in the battle with the lusts of our flesh and with the temptations of Satan has been completely secured at the cross of Jesus Christ. He won the battle for us!

Notice the outcome of this battle with the Amalekites:

> *Exodus 17:13 (NIV) So Joshua overcame the Amalekite army with the sword.*

Oh, yes, Joshua and the Israelites had to fight! They were down in the valley in the midst of the battle. But you can imagine them in the heat of the battle, looking up to the hill and seeing three men on it, and the one in the middle with arms raised was winning the battle for them!

We have to fight the battle with our flesh, the world, and Satan. The battle can get intense, but Jesus has conquered through death and resurrection. And you and I will overcome as we look up to that hill called Calvary.

> *"And having disarmed the powers and authorities, he made a public spectacle of them, triumphing over them by the cross"* (Colossians 2:15).

Suggested Songs
The Old Rugged Cross
Nailed to the Cross by Rend Collective
My Victory by Brenton Brown

Frequently Asked Questions

Question: If singleness is a gift then why is marriage encouraged? Isn't this contradictory? Isn't it better for us to be celibate instead of married?

Answer: Marriage is not the cure for sexual impurity, but the Scriptures say, *"Now to the unmarried and the widows I say: It is good for them to stay unmarried, as I do. <u>But if they cannot control themselves</u>, they should marry, for it is better to marry than to burn with passion."*

Physical intimacy within marriage is the only outlet that God has provided to us to satisfy sexual longings.

CPSIA information can be obtained
at www.ICGtesting.com
Printed in the USA
LVHW061023050920
665161LV00027B/2659

9 781733 760935